Praise for *Profit First for Creatives*

Profit First for Creatives ingeniously [...] to the distinct world of creative bus[iness. I]t arms the dreamers and makers wi[th the] wisdom they need to flourish without compromising their artistic integrity. Way to go, Christian, in writing a book for creatives that is based on your experiences.

Dennis Yu
author of *The Definitive Guide to TikTok Advertising*

No profit means you won't be able to sustain. If you want to do work that you care about and that matters to the world for a long time to come, *Profit First For Creatives* will show you the path.

Todd Henry
author of *The Brave Habit*

Profit First for Creatives explores the mindsets that often hold creative entrepreneurs back financially while charting a refreshing path to profitability.

John Jantsch
author of *Duct Tape Marketing*

To creative entrepreneurs, accounting jargon is as confusing as Swahili, and even less useful. That's why this book is a game-changer, knocking down barriers so those who love their craft can make a good living and pursue the work they love most.

Perry Marshall
author of *80/20 Sales and Marketing*

PROFIT FIRST
— FOR —
CREATIVES

Redefining the Creativity/Money Paradigm

CHRISTIAN BRIM, CPA, CMA

Copyright © 2024 by Christian Brim

Profit First for Creatives
Redefining the Creativity/Money Paradigm

All rights reserved.
No part of this work may be used or reproduced, transmitted, stored, or used in any form or by any means graphic, electronic, or mechanical, including but not limited to photocopying, recording, scanning, digitizing, taping, Web distribution, information networks or information storage and retrieval systems, or in any manner whatsoever without prior written permission from the publisher.
In this world of digital information and rapidly-changing technology, some citations do not provide exact page numbers or credit the original source. We regret any errors, which are a result of the ease with which we consume information.

Disclaimer: The material in this book represents the opinions of the author and may not be applicable to all situations. Accordingly, the author and publisher assume no responsibility for actions taken by readers based upon advice offered in this book. This book does not offer financial, business, or tax advice, each reader should use caution in applying any material contained in this book to their specific circumstance and should seek the advice of appropriate professionals. This book material contains advice on entrepreneurship and investing. Please be aware of the federal and state laws and tax regulations when considering the information shared in this book.

ISBN: (Paperback) 979-8-218-35165-6
Amazon ASIN: B0CW1BVR1L

"In the beginning, God created...
God created man in his own image."

You were made to create.

Table of Contents

Foreword ix
Introduction 1
    Chapter 1: Why You Are in This Situation 5
    Chapter 2: Profit First to the Rescue 23
    Chapter 3: Using Profit First to Increase Profit 37
    Chapter 4: Unlock Your Value with Pricing 55
    Chapter 5: Compare Yourself to Grow Yourself 71
    Chapter 6: Common Problems and Solutions 81
    Chapter 7: What Profit First Doesn't Do 91
    Chapter 8: Income Tax Strategies for Creatives 97
    Chapter 9: Advanced Concepts (HAM Chapter) 109
    Chapter 10: Final Thoughts 131
About the Author 134

Foreword

In my journey through the entrepreneurial battlefield—a realm where every day seems to be a skirmish, every decision a maneuver—I've seen the highs of victory (like, landing that big client) and the lows of defeat (like, not). It's a world I'm honored to immerse myself in, similar to a journalist reporting from a war zone. Here, amid the entrepreneurial hustle and the grind, one group consistently catches my eye—the creatives. Their struggle, their raw potential, and the world's need for creatives to be successful is exactly why I'm jazzed about Christian Brim's new book, *Profit First for Creatives*.

The consummate creative entrepreneur is brimming with ideas and overflowing with passion. But when it comes to the money part of the business? Well, that's where things get a bit dicey. It's a common scene, one I've witnessed countless times. These brilliant minds, often viewing profit as a pesky afterthought, end up in financial struggle. They're trying to juggle their art and their accounts, and let's be real—it's like mixing oil and water.

Enter Christian Brim. With his combo of CPA and CMA badges, and a career spanning over two decades, Christian doesn't just talk the talk, he walks the walk. His approach in *Profit First for Creatives* is a lifeline for the industry. Finally, in your hands, you have the simple "wonder weapon" to consistently win the daily financial battle overwhelming creatives.

We're living in a time where creativity isn't just a nice to have; it's the lifeblood of innovation. And yet, there's this crazy paradox—a decline in creativity just when we need it most. This is where Christian's playbook comes in. It's not about stifling creativity with financial strategies; it's about fueling it.

Reflecting on my own path, I have always thirsted for entrepreneurial ideas that make things work better, faster, and simpler. It has taken me decades to discover and deploy my best ideas. Christian's journey, from the high-flying corridors of Deloitte to the entrepreneurial trenches, mirrors this ethos. He's been in the thick of it, helping businesses, especially creative ones, find their footing.

Profit First for Creatives is more than just a build on my original *Profit First* concept. It's a beacon, a guiding light for the creative minds who've been groping in the dark, trying to figure out how to make their passion pay the bills. This book is Christian saying, "Hey, you can have your cake and eat it too. You can create and be profitable."

As you get ready to dig in, let me circle back to why this book hits the right notes for me. Being knee-deep in the entrepreneurial grind, I've always had a soft spot for the underdogs, the misfits, the creatives. They're the ones who often need just a nudge, a bit of know-how to turn their passion into a thriving business. Christian's book is that nudge. It's a game changer, a paradigm shifter. And it's an absolute honor to endorse it.

To each and every creative, struggling to make sense of the numbers—grab this book. It's your ticket to not just surviving in this wild entrepreneurial world but thriving in it. Christian Brim, you've nailed it, my friend.

Mike Michalowicz
author of *Profit First*

Introduction

The book *Profit First* was released in 2014 by Mike Michalowicz. I don't think Mike had any idea what it would become. It has sold over one million copies and has been translated into twenty-three languages. It has spawned a group of Profit First Professionals to assist business owners in implementing the Profit First method.

Mike's premise is deceivingly simple, and profoundly impactful. Over 600,000 businesses around the world have implemented the method and have found financial freedom. *Profit First* redefined the way business owners approach their finances.

This proven method simplifies your accounting to give you control and clarity about your business, while focusing on profit. Its powerful psychological principles work *with* your brain, not against it. Unlike traditional accounting processes, which are designed for reporting and compliance for large companies, the Profit First method doesn't require you, the business owner, to know anything about accounting to implement. The processes are structured in a way that doesn't require extensive financial understanding or training.

Profit First is useful for any business, but entrepreneurs in creative industries require a more nuanced approach, which is why I created the book you are reading. Thus, *Profit First for Creatives* is not just another Profit First derivative book.

First, it's important to explore what is meant by Creatives within the framework of Profit First. There are several Profit First books for specific industries, and they are great! However, when I approached Mike Michalowicz about the title, I was worried that the publisher wouldn't accept it. I worried that the name would be too vague. Was it for creative entrepreneurs or for entrepreneurs in creative industries, and if the latter, what businesses qualified as creative?

All of this led me to the question of who am I writing this book for? It is for entrepreneurs in creative industries.

- Videography
- Photography
- Cinematography
- Design
- Marketing agencies
- Interior designers
- Graphic designers
- Influencers and content creators

Essentially a creative industry is a business where you provide a service or product that is uniquely created for your customer.

What *Profit First for Creatives* became was a summary of everything I have learned so far about Profit First and small business finances. I've shared both success and failure. I've included real-world examples of clients and other creatives to assist you.

Along the way in writing this book, I had a profound discovery, and it is the core message of this book.

You don't have to compromise your creativity to make a profit. Creativity and profitability are complementary!

My name is Christian Brim. I'm a Certified Public Accountant and Certified Management Accountant. My bona fides include working with hundreds of businesses over the course of my thirty-year career helping them with their money. I have been married to Stacey for thirty years, and we have three adult children. I mention this only because those relationships have shaped who I am as a professional. I have the experience of success and failure, of perseverance to chase my passion, and of helping folks like you be successful.

This book is a guide to profitability just for business owners like you. My hope is that you will read it, contemplate it, and then use it.

Reading this book will no more make your business finances improve than if you read a book on how to play golf and join the PGA. You will have to go the driving range and practice.

This book will introduce you to the Profit First concepts and how to implement them in your creative business. More importantly, we will unpack the mindset issues that keep creatives struggling financially.

Grabbing hold of the core concept that you can be both creative and profitable, you will begin your journey to financial calm. I want everyone to have the peace that one Profit First client described:

"The Profit First model just changed everything for me, and it's given me so much clarity. I'm now able to operate the business and not worry about money, just have a clear vision of finance and how my business needs to make money for me first before it does anything else."

That is my hope for each of you!

In Chapter 1, I discuss the mindset of creatives regarding money and finance. To me, it is foundational and potentially the most valuable chapter in the book. Chapter 2 discusses the Profit First method and how to get started. Chapter 3 shows you how to use the method to improve your profit, which continues into Chapter 4 where we discuss value pricing, your most powerful tool.

Chapter 5 gives you sample information by industry for comparison, and Chapter 6 deals with common problems in implementing Profit First. In Chapter 7, we discuss the additional processes you need in support of Profit First, while Chapter 8 gives you my favorite tax strategies for creatives.

Chapter 9 is for the small percentage of you that want to go HAM (if you don't know the term, it is an acronym for Hard as a Mother-$uck@r).

Let's go!

Chapter 1:
You Have a Problem

Chris is like most creatives. He has a videography business that aims to connect people with brands. Before reading *Profit First*, Chris had several expenses paid to subcontractors prior to receiving payment from his customers. Tracking this money and staying within the project budget were constant struggles. Chris describes it this way. "I had no idea what to do with my money and had no idea where it was going. I felt like I didn't know what to do."

Similarly, Evan, a twelve-year cinematographer, struggled with cash flow management. He struggled with paying himself consistently. Evan describes his pre-Profit First life as largely chaotic and unorganized. Sound familiar?

If you're like Chris and Evan, you started your business to pursue your creative passion, and making money was secondary. It wasn't that you didn't think you needed to make money. You knew you had to feed yourself and your family, of course! But making money and profitability, bookkeeping, taxes, licenses, and all that other stuff, if it was on your radar, it was *way* down the list of priorities. Let's look at another example.

Nick owns a video production house and has been in business for over five years. He echoed the same things as Chris, "With our business, when we first started out, we were spending a lot just from investing in gear or projects. We were finding in that beginning phase that we weren't really taking a lot home at the end of the day. So how do we change that? We're not doing this purely just so we can *spend* money."

Like every creative who starts a business, the "business" stuff just seems to get in the way. It's a necessary evil that you put to the back burner, until that pot boils over, and you have a real mess on your hands. This is where Profit First comes in.

Profit First is a simple method to organize your finances and ensure profitability. We'll dive into the process in Chapter 2, but in summary, Profit First is simple to implement:

1. Open the five bank accounts (Deposit, Profit, Taxes, Owner's Compensation, Operating Expenses). (Chapter 2)
2. Do an Instant Profit Assessment. (Chapter 3)
3. Use your Instant Profit Assessment to establish your Target Allocation Percentages (TAPs). (Chapters 3 and 5)
4. Deposit all of your income into the Deposit account. (Chapter 2)
5. Periodically (e.g., twice a month) transfer money from the Deposit account to the other accounts using your TAPs. (Chapter 2)
6. Distribute your profit to yourself once a quarter. (Chapter 2)
7. Evaluate your TAPs for the next quarter. (Chapter 2)

This Chapter is to help you understand the following:

1. You have a problem.
2. Why you are in this situation.
3. How to change it.

My Story

Although I am not in a creative industry, I am a creative entrepreneur. A creative entrepreneur is one driven by passion, as opposed to by opportunity.

If the previous statement describes you, then my story will be very familiar. I grew up in a family business in small town Oklahoma. My dad, his brothers, and my grandfather were in the oil field service business. I saw firsthand the joys and heartaches of being an entrepreneur and its impact on the family.

Weekends were spent all together at someone's house. My cousins and I would swim and play games for hours, while the adults "talked." Most of the time the talk turned to work. First lesson, it's almost impossible to separate work from family. Looking back, I see how they just couldn't escape it. Their troubles followed them home, and because they worked together, their family problems followed them to work. Lesson two, if you work with family, it makes things more difficult.

Then came an economic calamity. We went from flying in private aircraft and riding in limousines to living in a rented house and driving shitty cars. I was seventeen at the time. In retrospect, it wasn't the loss of things that really bothered me.

No, the worst part of financial failure was the emotional effect it had on my family. Around the same time our family suffered financial calamity, my grandmother died of lung cancer (literally smoking a cigarette on her death bed). She was the matriarch of the family, and with her death, the glue holding us together was gone. After filing bankruptcy, everyone left the state to find work. Gone were the halcyon days of family togetherness.

My dad found employment in upstate New York in the Native American gaming business. He worked there my senior year, while the rest of us stayed in Oklahoma. My mother and siblings dropped me off at college and left. Not left me, left the state. I had a few friends from high school, but other than that, I might as well have gone to school far away.

I decided on accounting as a major because I liked math, and engineers worked way too hard. Accounting was the hardest major in the school of business, so I picked that, thinking it would be easier to find a job after graduation. I had no idea what accounting was.

I graduated, met a nice girl (Stacey, my wife of thirty years), we married, and she became pregnant on our honeymoon. NO idea how that happened. I actually do, but I won't bother you with the details. I took work with a Big 4 accounting firm as an auditor. After two years of travel away from my young family, I looked for something else.

I wanted to do something more in sales because I like helping people. I went to work for a small community bank as a commercial banker. That was very interesting, but it created my life-long disdain for bankers. After we were acquired by a larger bank, I again started looking for something else.

Since I was a kid, I have been fascinated by the stock market. I had dreams of being an investment banker (again, had no idea what that was) just like the movie *Wall Street*. No, not *The Wolf of Wall Street*, the one in the '80s with Kirk and Michael Douglas. So, I decided I would give it a try.

I was rejected by every single brokerage house. The last straw was when one of them gave me a sales aptitude test and said they could not hire me even if they wanted to with my scores. I literally laughed out loud. I had no doubt of my ability to sell, even at that young age.

What do you do when God closes one door? I looked for an open one. In the *Journal of Accountancy*, I saw an ad for an accounting franchise business. Curious, I looked at their website (this was 1996 and the internet was in its infancy). I contacted the sales director, who was from Dallas, and whose wife was from Oklahoma City, where I then lived. We made an instant connection.

I did my due diligence, which really only consisted of talking to other franchisees and confirming what I wanted to hear. But I really liked the idea that I would be able to help business owners with their money. As a banker, I had seen the mess their books were in. I did not really understand it then, but my motivation was to exorcise the ghosts of my family. I knew that business owners did not have to work their asses off and then end up with nothing.

Next, I had to find the money to pay the franchise fee. It was $40k, and we had nothing. I asked my father-in-law to loan me the money, and he said no. He was the only relative I had with that kind of coin. So on to plan B, the Small Business Administration. Remember, I was a banker!

Long story short, I borrowed $50k from the SBA, ran up my credit cards doing the three-week training in Southern California, and I was off. When you have no alternatives, you find a way to make it work. I spent most of my days cold calling businesses in person, and then following up on the phone to arrange appointments. I had nothing else to do, I had no clients.

It didn't take long to find my first clients, and Stacey started doing bookkeeping while nursing our newborn. Yes, we had another child two years after the first. What the hell? So, I did the marketing and occasional taxes while Stacey answered the phone and did the books.

Looking back, it was a crazy decision, one I am unsure I would make again. I had no alternatives except success or bankruptcy, and I had four mouths to feed. Well technically three since our daughter preferred breast milk, but my wife was eating for two.

At that time, I was in the same boat as Chris. New business, young family, selling like crazy to make sure we were successful. But what next? The money came in, then what? You would think that CPAs are good bookkeepers, but we are not. In fact, we make awful bookkeepers.

I'd like to tell you that I implemented Profit First and lived happily ever after. The book and Mike were some years in the future, so I did what everyone else does: I sold more. I grew the business. Profit was not really a priority. That didn't work so well. (I will discuss that in Chapter 9 in the section Building a Business.)

Like me and Chris, you would be happy if your business made money while doing what you love. Or to put it in terms of creatives, I would be happy if my business made money without compromising my creative integrity.

Maybe you feel like Nick, our owner of a video production house.

"Just getting a ton of money isn't going to actually make me feel like it's going well. If the work isn't fulfilling in some way, I would rather start taking on some jobs that fulfill me creatively more than only the ones that are going to pay the bills. It's weird that you have to kind of convince yourself to take a project that isn't fulfilling for you just to make more money."

Or maybe your business is already making a profit, just not enough. John Jantsch, author of *Duct Tape Marketing,* was in that situation.

"I thought that for tax purposes we wouldn't want to show a profit. But at some point, we are going to want to sell the business. And it dawned on me that we are not able to show it, even though we are making a profit, because it's not in the traditional fashion. For whatever reason, I think a lot of people experience this. The shift is sort of magical and it has us focused on profit, and so, inevitably, our profit is greater. Now we do other things to make sure that **everything we do is profitable**."

Unfortunately, far too many businesses are not profitable. The path of business ownership is littered with the corpses of creatives that failed. Out of fear, they took whatever work they could find, just to keep the lights on. They compromised on their passion, their dream, just to make a buck. All the while, slowly dying inside. This is not what you signed up for!

But what if you didn't have to sacrifice profit for creativity? What if you could do what you loved, and were paid well for it?

Here is the truth:

You don't have to compromise your creativity to make a profit. Creativity and profitability are complementary!

Remember Chris the videographer and how he felt before implementing Profit First? Implementing Profit First, he was able to have predictable cash flow, which gave him the space and freedom to work on his business creativity. How did he feel after implementing Profit First?

According to Chris,

"I think a huge struggle an artist has is not being a very good bookkeeper or accountant and they just struggle. It's the classic feast or famine.

"When down months happened, which for me, usually it's December, January, February, around the holidays, I wasn't very creative. I panic more than anything, just trying to just obsess over finding work and the creativity goes out the door.

"The challenge kept me from being creative and it kept me from accepting the right work. It kept me in panic mode. I was accepting work that was way too cheap, which kept me way too busy. And I could not ever think about growing my business, or working on my business, I was just stuck in this work.

"With Profit First, I'm able to decline cheap jobs that I shouldn't do, which opens up time to accept those jobs that are larger ticket. **And the more profitable I am, the more creative I am.**"

Todd Henry, author of *The Accidental Creative,* has a very interesting perspective on this, as well as a warning.

Henry asserted in an interview that:

"One of the things where I think we do a lot of damage to people is when we give them advice like 'Figure out something you love, and you'll never work a day in your life.' I think that's very damaging advice because reality is, and we all know this, when you find something you love, you're going to work a lot in order to see that outcome achieved. And it will feel like work.

"The root of the word passion is the word *pessio*, which means to suffer. So, when we say follow your passion, what we're really telling people is follow your suffering. It doesn't quite have the same ring to it, but what it means is find the thing that you care so much about that you're willing, if necessary, to suffer to see it achieved.

"That doesn't mean you will suffer. Sometimes it'll bring you alive. Sometimes you'll feel like you're on cloud nine, but you're willing, if necessary, to suffer because the outcome matters more to you than your temporary suffering. That's the thing that's going to lead to profit in the long run, because you're going to wade through things other people aren't willing to in order to achieve that outcome."

You purchased and are reading this book because you thought you might have a money problem. Like most creatives, you struggle with how to make money in your business without compromising your profitability. Let's look at why creatives are in this collective situation.

Why You Are in Your Current Situation

After talking to at least one hundred creative entrepreneurs in all types of businesses, from videographers to marketing agencies, I've discovered three common mindset issues. These have to be addressed before moving to fixing your financial situation. These three problems are as follows:

- Balancing Passion with the Type of Work (The 3-Prong Decision of Creatives)
- Feelings of Low Self-Worth (You are Worth It!)
- Not Having Good Financial Habits (Get Your Personal House in Order)

1. The 3-Prong Decision of Creatives

The first common reason creatives struggle with profitability is the complication of balancing our passion with the type of work we perform. Every business has to balance two things: what the customer will pay for the work, and what it costs the business to produce the work. This is the profit paradigm we all must follow. Creatives, however, add a third element: whether they want to do the work.

Most non-creatives don't even consider this aspect. They only ask, "Can the business make a profit given what the customer will pay?" Whether they should actually *do* the work doesn't even cross their minds.

I was at an event with master marketer and author Perry Marshall (*80/20 Marketing*), who described the two different types of entrepreneurs. He said there were builders and artists. Builders see an opportunity in the market and a way to make money. They are not particularly concerned with what the business is, rather that there is opportunity.

Meanwhile, an artist entrepreneur follows their passion and builds a business around it. They see the same opportunities as the builder but aren't interested because the opportunities aren't lined up with their passion. I had never had this dynamic explained in such a way. It was eye-opening!

The world has enough opportunistic people, enough builders. What we lack is creatives: People driven by passion—people who see needs in the marketplace, and want to help people, not just make money. (By the way, I think it is really a continuum with builders on one end and artists on the other, with money and passion. Both builders and artists have both passion and a profit motivation, but to differing degrees. And neither is right or wrong.)

Of course, to be able to innovate with passion and help others, you do have to run a profitable business. Thus, *Profit First for Creatives* allows you to change this dynamic so that you *can* balance all three elements.

Jon, an Emmy-award-winning sports producer of eight years, did it.

"I absolutely love sports and I can make a lot of money doing it. It's a win-win. I don't need to sacrifice money, or I don't need to sacrifice my creative side because this fulfills both.

"You're going to have challenges no matter what markets you do business in. That's been my journey over the years. Finding my market, finding my niche, finding what I really wanted to do where hopefully I could make money and also enjoy the work. So, the sports market has been the answer for me to that. But I know a lot of people and creatives who don't have that."

You can be like Jon. Implementing Profit First improves your profit and gives you clarity on your financial situation, by enabling you to organize and automate your financials, so you can focus on your creative output. That leads to less stress and worry, which in turn allows you to work on your business to make it even better. You can do what Jon did and focus on a specific niche (one that inspires you) and go even deeper with your customers.

Or consider Michael's (another sports videographer) take. "The passion and the artwork alone, it is important, but it's equally important in my opinion just to know long-term, financially, what this is all about so you can keep doing it."

As we've established, Profit First is a mind shift created by Mike Michalowicz, and it's an amazing tool for helping businesses solve the problem of profitability. His Profit First Professional group's motto is "Eliminating Entrepreneurial Poverty." It is a tool to use, but more importantly, a different way of thinking.

The method is simple and intuitive. It meets you where you are and doesn't expect you to have an understanding of accounting, bookkeeping, or taxes. Too many creatives reluctantly work with an accounting professional, not having a clue what they are being told. Because Profit First enables you to organize and automate your finances, you are free to be creative. At the end of the day, the old accounting model doesn't serve you. It serves the accountant and the government. It does nothing to help ensure that your business serves *your* needs.

As Jon puts it,

"I mean, before Profit First, my business was pretty disorganized from a financial workflow standpoint. I liked Profit First because it was a system that I could grasp, because I'm a pretty straightforward thinker. I'm not highly financially technical.

"Before Profit First, I would have $15,000 in the account, but I knew that $4,000 of it was coming out to pay my contractors for this shoot coming up. Then I knew that I actually had about $11,000, but then I had another job come in. So, then the bank balance went up, and I had more expenses coming out.

"I had to try to remember I had $4,000 of expense from this other one, and then I've got $2,500 worth of expense for the second one. So then, how much money do I actually have to cover overhead? That's the cycle that I was in. The mental toll of trying to figure out how I can keep enough money aside for things like rent and internet and utilities. It got very, very messy, very quickly.

"So Profit First really alleviated just about all of that stress of not knowing how much I had, because I reorganized everything. I've got the operating expense account, I have a contractor's account, I have the profit account, I have all these different accounts so that things can be more separated and organized so then that way I know, okay, I don't touch any of the money in the contractor's account, I don't touch any of the money in the tax account."

Because Jon implemented Profit First, his bank accounts were organized, and because he knew how much money there was to spend, it removed a lot of the stress around money. How easy is it to be creative when you're stressed? It's not. In fact, it's almost impossible to be creative when you're stressed and distracted—something Profit First aims to alleviate.

Of course, it's worth noting that creativity doesn't always result in profitability, but sustained profitability requires creativity. We do creative things all the time without expectation of a financial reward. That is who we are and what we do. There is absolutely nothing wrong with this. The question is this: How can you harness this creativity to produce profit? Profitability can happen by accident, but continuous profit requires continuous creativity.

But that creativity may come in ways that you may be unused to. Consider Jaren's case, a twelve-year veteran of music videos.

"I had to redirect my creative energy and be creative in a different way. In order to be profitable or sustainable, what I am doing today may not reap a benefit today. It may be six months from now.

"Sometimes, in order to get there, you have to do the things that maybe are not your passion or that you don't particularly care about to make the money to get to that space. For example, I once shot (videoed!) a president. Had I not done all the regular non-sexy things leading up to that, I would have never even gotten asked to be in that room.

"To be sustainable for creatives long-term, you have to recognize you can't put all your eggs in one basket.

"People who sell Christmas trees aren't selling Christmas trees year-round. They have to figure out other things to keep them profitable for the rest of the year. It made me realize that a lot of creatives become fixated on, here's the thing I like doing.

"Someone may say they like creating music videos. They like doing whatever it may be. And then... after six months when the business has died down or fizzled out or the excitement is gone, they say that it's not working out, and they are going to go back to work. What's not working out is that they weren't getting creative with their business. They weren't creating other opportunities to make money."

Does that sound like you? If so, then trust that by the end of this book, you will have the tools to make a profit in your creative business without compromising who you are as a creative. In fact, it's just the opposite. As your profitability grows, so will your creativity, as you've seen from those who have implemented Profit First and shared their stories in this chapter.

While you may be at a point where you feel frustrated, don't lose heart. Believe me—the world needs creative entrepreneurs like you. In fact, it is desperate for you. We need more out-of-the-box thinkers to solve the challenging problems we face. We need people who are passionate about their cause, a passion only creatives bring.

My passion has always been about helping business owners. I can wake up, do it all day, and not feel tired. I've tried other things both in business and outside. I started a software company, thinking that would scratch my itch. After all, everyone else seemed to be doing it. I tried all kinds of personal distractions. I ran a marathon, completed an Iron Man triathlon, became a private pilot, joined a country club (twice). I tried more spiritual endeavors like going on a mission trip and doing reading tutoring through my church. In the end, *nothing* stoked that fire like sitting with a struggling business owner and helping them have clarity as to their problems and guiding them to solutions. Seeing them overcome with relief when they made it through their situation—*that* is what the world needs—people with that level of commitment to their purpose.

Before we pick up the tool that is Profit First, we must address mindset. A tool is only useful in the hands of the right person. Put a hammer in my hand, and I'm just as likely to end up with bent nails and bruised thumbs as I am to connect two things.

Before you use the tool, you have to understand what it was designed for and how to best use it for your purposes. You have to understand its limitations, what it can't do, and how it shouldn't be used. Ever try to hammer in a screw? Or screw in a nail? To put it a different way, you have to know what the tool is *intended* to do. Profit First is intended to help your business be profitable, sustainable, less stressful, and more fulfilling. It is designed to give you back control of your business and make it serve you, rather than the other way around.

Before we implement the tool, we have to look at this question of profit. Many creatives feel like *profit* is a dirty word. That somehow if you make money, you've sold out. You've compromised somewhere. Maybe you grew up in a home where money was scarce, or not even discussed. You may have learned a lot of things that you've found do not fit reality. In some ways, you are going to have to unlearn what you know to move forward.

You can implement Profit First, and it will help with all of the things I've mentioned. If you don't take control of your intent, your mindset about profit and money, you will be unsuccessful. If you don't think that you deserve to be paid well for your creativity, you won't. If you believe that making money as a creative means you must compromise who you are, then *that* will be your reality.

Simon Sinek, famous author of *Start with Why*, popularized (although its origins are uncertain) the phrase, "How you do anything is how you do everything." For us, that means that how you think about money, and how you handle it in your personal life, is how you will handle it in your business. You can't just put on a figurative new hat when you start a business and suddenly think differently about money and profit.

To summarize, the idea that you have to do work you don't want to do to make a profit is false. Your profit is directly tied to your creativity.

2. You Are Worth It!

Most creatives don't come into business with a strong business or financial background, but we *all* have learned things about money. We all bring assumptions, prejudices, and values to the table. Let's address the most basic: You are worth it.

My childhood was spent in a blended family. I had four younger siblings from a different mother. My parents only had me. I spent most of my time with my dad, stepmother, and my siblings. Although I was the oldest, because I spent time visiting my mother, it was clear that I was different from them. In the way only children can do, I was belittled as only being "half." I didn't realize how deeply this affected me long into adulthood. I had a strong feeling of not being sufficient, not being enough. I was somehow deficient or incomplete.

Maybe you have a similar situation where a parent, teacher, or coach taught you that you were not worthy. I am not a therapist and I'm not going to try and resolve those issues here but know that until you address your self-worth, you are limiting yourself. Many creatives have been told their work is not "real work." I'm not talking about being a pseudo-optimist who says, "I know I'm good enough," I'm talking about really digging into the reasons you believe what you do, and how you feel. I'm talking about knowing your tremendous value.

Until you feel worthy of being paid more, you will be on the struggle bus of profitability.

You can be like Kyle, a director of photography and drone pilot. Before implementing Profit First, his work was sporadic, working fifteen days one month and four the next. Income predictability and stability were a constant challenge.

"The hardest part was getting to the point where I believed I was worth that amount of money per day to make that salary.

"Working with my Profit First Professional, Jeremy at Core Group, we set a goal. We set a standard. Now, how do I create that standard in my world? It's been the way I've dealt with that instability of my whole thinking that the invoice is my labor *plus* my gear. And I can make it work out for the bills this month.

"It's helped me stand on my rate. No, you need to pay me this first, the gear and all this stuff is after that. So, it's really helped my mindset in that way, **knowing what I'm worth and going for it.**

"It was a little bit of a transition, but it was more of *reframing in my brain* how I saw the value of me and my work, not just my work as a whole. I work six days a month at my full labor rate to pay my salary. That's been life changing."

You can see from Kyle's story that mindset was the game changer regarding his ability to be both profoundly creative and simultaneously profitable.

There are a lot of ways you can look at money. Because money is pervasive in our lives, many problems or feelings that you *think* are about money, really aren't. You could line one hundred people up and get one hundred different opinions and values about money, like what is important, what to do with it, how to use it.

I prefer the Orthodox biblical view that money is a tool given to us by God to fulfill our divine purpose. It is neither good nor bad, intrinsically—rather it is what you do with it that matters.

If you are fulfilling your purpose (passion/dreams) then you should expect profit/success to flow from it. It is confirmation that you are doing what you are supposed to do. In more secular, practical terms, if your business doesn't make a profit, then you are a philanthropist. Nothing wrong with that at all, but you are in business to make a profit. Hard stop.

To make Profit First work optimally for you, you need to reframe your internal conversation about money and profit to one where profit allows you to fulfill more of your purpose. Regardless of what you may have learned and whatever it is that your business does, you are 100 percent worth whatever you charge for your services.

3. Get Your Personal House in Order

Last, if you make your business profitable, but you don't control your personal finances, you are walking around with a leaky bucket. It doesn't matter how much you put into the top of it, you will always run out.

It is important to determine a profitability expectation/goal for you and your dependents. Although you may not start where you want, your goal gives you a target when we move into the Profit First implementation (see Chapter 3).

Some creatives use a modified Profit First method for their personal finances. They allocate a percentage of their income to investment or other financial goals (saving for a house, reducing debt), and then live on the rest. You can even go old school like Mike suggests in *Profit First* and use the envelope system his grandmother used. Cash goes into specific envelopes (groceries, entertainment) with each payday, and when that envelope is empty, you are done spending that month.

In order for Profit First to work for you, you will have to make sure your personal financial house is in order.

How Do You Change Your Situation?

First and foremost, in order to implement Profit First, you have to change your mindset about profit. Profitability is driven by creativity. How does a business make money? It creates value for others at a cost that is less than they charge. Not complicated. The more value a company creates the more money they can charge.

Gail Doby, founder of The Pearl Collective, a company that helps interior designers scale their businesses, puts it very well.

"So, creativity is to me the bedrock of what we do. And quite frankly, as a business owner, I come from a finance background, but I also have a design degree. So, I have a right and left brain. But what I have found is the creative part is the edge that most businesses have. If you're good at creativity and you're good at creatively solving problems, you're probably going to win over your competitors because of your viewpoint and your thinking process."

Think of Apple. When they created their iPhone, it was truly novel. Nothing like it had ever existed before. Billions of dollars in profit later, it still commands a hefty price and a staggering profit. Apple is uber-focused on their customers and their experience. Simon Sinek's famous Ted Talk covers how Apple communicates from their Why, which is to make beautiful technology products that are easy to use. Now, whether that is true or not (I'm an Android user so it's not true for me) it doesn't matter. They have created products that solve a problem for their customers, and they love them.

We will cover this more in detail in Chapter 4 when we discuss the pricing of your services but do consider that the more you deliver value to your customers, the more profit you will earn. Just like Jaren and Apple, you have to answer the question, "How do I create more value?" Simple: creativity. You create a solution to solve your customer's problem. When you create a truly unique solution, you can charge whatever you want and in turn, drive a profitable business that enables you to pursue your passion with relative abandon.

Profitability isn't just about providing financial stability for you and your family. You can do that with a traditional job, working for someone else. A business must be profitable for its own sake, beyond what you pay yourself, to be truly sustainable. Your business should have sufficient cash reserves so that if something were to happen to you, the wheels won't fall off.

Think about it: If all the business does is pay you a reasonable salary, it's not a business, it's a job, just one where you happen to set some of the terms. We will discuss why your business needs more revenue than just that which is needed to pay you in more depth in Chapter 9 when we discuss Building Your Business to Sell. Consider—what happens if you are sick or injured? Can the business make money without you? Can it make a profit? If you have a business, the answer is yes.

Most business owners will not commit to the work to make their business self-sufficient beyond themselves. Some will and will be even closer to fulfilling their passion.

Summary

You agree that you have a business that needs to get its financial house in order, and that you have to address your mindset about money, regardless of what you have known or thought in the past. You understand that you are worth what you charge, and that most importantly, profit is directly tied to your creativity. You believe that your business *has* to make a profit in order to survive and thrive.

In the next chapter, we will discuss, with Profit First, how you can do exactly that.

Action item: Open a savings account for profit. Take 1 percent of *every* deposit and put it in the profit account. If you do *nothing* else, this small step will have a huge effect!

Chapter 2:
Profit First to the Rescue

When I first heard Mike Michalowicz's story sometime shortly after he published his book in 2014, he was speaking at an Entrepreneurs' Organization event in Oklahoma City. Mike is a great storyteller. If you haven't heard his story, *Profit First* is worth buying just to read it. The quick version is this. Mike created two businesses early in his life. The businesses didn't make much money while he was growing them, but he sold them for some bucks.

He became an angel investor, taking his bankroll and investing in startup businesses. He failed miserably, losing everything. Sitting, watching TV, and eating potato chips, he was in a very dark place. From that place, he started to rethink what he had done, and how he could do it differently. This led him on a journey that eventually became Profit First.

In this chapter, I will discuss in detail the principles of Profit First that drive the structure of the process and the basic parts of the method.

Principles of Profit First

There are some basic concepts of Profit First. Understanding them will make the implementation easier. You don't need to do a deep dive into each of these psychological principles unless they don't ring true to you. Then, by all means, do your own research. Just know that these principles are practical, not just conceptual. They are tried and true across tens of thousands of businesses that have implemented Profit First. If you find yourself bucking up against one of them, lean into it.

Question why those feelings come up, and make sure you've come to terms with them before moving forward. You don't have to be an evangelist for the cause at this point, but as you will see when we talk about common problems in implementation in Chapter 6, when you stumble implementing Profit First, it will likely tie back to one of these principles. Make sure you understand them and accept their importance.

1. Use Small Plates (Parkinson's Law)

The first principle is Use Small Plates, based upon Parkinson's Law. Defined by historian C. Northcot Parkinson in 1955, Parkinson's Law is the observation that work expands to fill the allotted time. Although the work Parkinson did was around public administration, you see this play out in various ways throughout the history of human behavior. When you have a deadline, you meet it. The same principle applies to money.

As we've already discussed, one of the priorities of your business is to make a profit. How we apply Parkinson's Law in Profit First is we limit the amount of money that is available to spend. If the cash isn't there, you can't spend it. Mike Michalowicz used the phrase Use Small Plates. When you are trying to lose weight, you use a smaller plate to ensure that you are taking proper portions. Big plates hold more food. We want to remove the big plate, and the temptation to spend it, thus the use of different bank accounts.

2. Serve Sequentially (Prioritize)

The second principle is Serve Sequentially, based upon the Primacy Effect. Our brains are hardwired for several things. Most of the time this serves us well, but those things can also be limitations. One of the beautiful things about Profit First is it works *with* your tendencies, that hard wiring.

The Primacy Effect is our cognitive bias to remember and focus on the information we receive first. What do we put first? Profit. This may seem like a small thing, but it really isn't. A common response to people who have not implemented Profit First, is "we're not making any money/profit" so we can't do Profit First. They have it completely backward. You don't have any profit *because* you're not making Profit First!

If profit isn't the *first* thing, it will *always* be secondary. Read that again. Until you commit to making profit *first*, there will *always* be reasons you don't have any.

Michalowicz equates this to filling your plate with the good stuff first (he must like to eat). Put the vegetables on your plate first, then fill in with the yummy stuff. Set aside profit first, and then you can "eat" what's left.

3. Remove Temptation

The third principle is Remove Temptation. I don't know about you, but my wife and I frequently find ourselves lying in bed at night asking the question, "Is there anything sweet in the house?" Usually the answer is no, and you know what, we don't get dressed and go down to the 7-Eleven to get something sweet. Why? The temptation is not readily available. Now if there is ice cream in the freezer, you can bet one of us is going to the kitchen.

James Clear, in his book *Atomic Habits,* talks about making habits easier. Our brains are lazy. They take the path of least resistance. The goal is to make your new money habit as easy to follow as possible. One way we do this is by making the alternative difficult.

Profit First does this by putting profit in a separate bank account with no online access, so that it is not available to spend or transfer to your other accounts. When you run out of money for the month, dipping into your profit account isn't so simple. You can't just transfer the amount online.

Some people go even further, requiring a second signature on the profit account, adding another circuit breaker. If you have to go get your business partner or spouse to sign a check to move money, it's not going to be easy. Of course, setting the money aside upfront also is a way of removing temptation.

Even if you have a great deal of self-control around money, this method will make it both easy and uncomplicated to allocate funds according to their designated purpose. At minimum, it saves you time and effort regarding your business expenditures. At best, it saves you money because you're not using funds needed elsewhere for something else.

To summarize, there are three overarching principles that are the foundation of Profit First.

- Use small plates (Parkinson's Law) by separating your money into separate bank accounts.
- Serve sequentially to prioritize your money. Profit is always first.
- Remove temptation by separating profit so that you don't spend it.

The Profit First Process

The Profit First Process or method consists of three things: Bank Accounts, Transfers/Allocations, and Establishing a Rhythm. Let's start with bank accounts, the foundation of the whole thing.

1. Bank Accounts

There are five business bank accounts associated with Profit First. I've added two additional for creatives that are optional, but highly recommended.

1. Deposit/Income
2. Profit
3. Tax
4. Owner's Compensation
5. Operating Expenses (OpEx)
6. Contractors
7. Payroll

Deposit

This is the account where all of your money comes in. You may be tempted to skip this account, but don't. You need a place to "stage" your money, so that you can properly allocate it. If you try to do this in another account, it will just complicate things. Somebody might say,

I don't need this account; I'll just put all my deposits into the Profit account and transfer everything from there.

There is an important mental practice you are doing by having a deposit account. You are saying this is the amount of profit and transferring it to the separate account. You are allocating it *up front*, setting it aside, paying yourself first. If you don't have a deposit account and work from your profit account, you will be that much more tempted to use that profit.

Additionally, you can easily look at your deposits in this account for any date range and see how much revenue came into the business. How much revenue have you had this year? It only takes a second to get that answer.

Last, because only deposits go into this account, you can easily see if something is coming out of your bank that shouldn't be. Maybe it's a return item on a check you deposited, or a disputed credit card charge. Very helpful!

Profit

Once you make a deposit, you will transfer a percentage of it into the profit account. We'll go into more detail in the next chapter about how to determine the percentage. Your rhythm of when you make the transfers may differ. Some people do it once a week, while others do it twice a month. I recommend starting to do a profit transfer with *each* deposit. Remember, you're building new habits here!

The profit account should be a savings account, to limit the activity (another removing temptation item). I recommend that you *not* have online access to this account. Out of sight, out of mind, although with some banks, not having online access may make the transfers more cumbersome. Don't let the ideal keep you from starting the habit!

Tax

I've seen more businesses go under from not paying taxes than I care to remember. After taking your profit, setting aside your tax on that profit is critical. You don't want to be struggling in March or April to figure out how to pay your taxes. Too much stress!

Again, we will discuss the amount that will be allocated to the tax account later. Your percentage should be customized to your tax situation. You can discuss with your tax preparer to help you estimate the percentage amount. It is better to allocate too much than too little, so be conservative in your estimate, and check in with your tax adviser during the year to make sure your estimate is on track.

This account only deals with your personal income taxes. Other taxes (e.g., property tax) will be paid through the OpEx account.

Owner's Compensation
Many businesses implementing Profit First skip this account, and in some cases, that's okay. Remember the Serve Sequentially principle above? First profit, then taxes, and now you pay yourself. I can't emphasize this enough, but you have to make sure you pay yourself a predictable, sustainable amount. Owner's compensation is what you are paying yourself.

I was a complete asshole when my business was younger. I actually didn't pay myself until my wife came and asked me for money. This is *not* how to run your business or your family finances!

Discussing this with Kyle (our director of photography), his light-bulb moment when he knew that Profit First was working was when he started seeing paychecks come in.

"My business needs to **make money for me first** before it does anything else.

"What guarantee do I have that my paycheck is coming in two weeks? Knowing that the money is coming to me before it goes to the business has reframed how I run the business. If I've had a slow month, just knowing that in two weeks that same salary number is coming, and that I framed my lifestyle around that number lets me rest easy at night. That's super important for the psyche."

Wow!

If you are paying yourself as an employee from your business, you can alternatively use the payroll account for this. Regardless, the point is to *pay yourself!*

Extra: Consider forming an LLC before you create your bank accounts. See Chapter 8 Tax Strategies.

Operating Expenses (OpEx)
This is the account to pay all of your expenses, except your pay and your income taxes. If you have a business credit card, it is paid from here.

It is uber-critical to *not* pay personal expenses from this account. Good financial hygiene requires separation of all business expenses into a separate account. If you have personal credit cards, mortgages, utility bills, or any other personal expenses coming from this account, you are asking for financial trouble, not to mention a tax enema.

Those are the five basic accounts to implement Profit First. If you haven't already set up your profit account, do it today, now.

Optional (but Recommended) Accounts

Although these two accounts are not officially part of the Profit First process, I recommend that you use them. Understand, they are not required; they are optional. If you are unsure about your situation, don't start with them and add them later. I don't want the decision whether to have these accounts or not to keep you from setting up the five primary accounts and starting to use Profit First.

Many industries have found that because of the specific requirements in their businesses they need additional bank accounts. Creatives are no different. These additional bank accounts are frequently used in creative industries to provide additional control, organization, and clarity.

1. Contractors

The first optional account I recommend is for contractor payments. If you use independent contractors, subcontractors, or equipment rental for a project, it is best to keep these payments separate. In a very real sense, this is not your money.

Michalowicz discusses a trap that some businesses fall into, usually construction companies, where they have a ton of flow-through expenses. They may have a $1M revenue company, but 50 percent of that goes to contractors. They really have a $500,000 company, not a million-dollar company.

Thinking about your business this way will pay dividends in the future. For instance, does it make sense to hire someone in-house for a contractor expense you consistently have? Should you purchase equipment that you are constantly renting? By *not* considering this as your income, only working with what is truly your income, you clarify the decision. More on that later.

2. Payroll

I discuss the powerful tax strategy of S-Corporations in Chapter 8. If you choose this strategy, you will need to pay yourself as a W-2 employee. And if you have employees, even if it is only yourself, receiving a W-2 wage, I recommend a payroll account. Nonpayment of payroll taxes and errors in filing of payroll returns is the number one target for the Internal Revenue Service, and many businesses have gone down from this. If you don't have an S-Corporation and don't have any employees, you will pay yourself from the owner's compensation account.

If you are using a payroll service, use this account. Transfer the entire cash requirement prior to each payroll from operating expense account (OpEx). If you are doing your payroll yourself, do the same thing, but the balance will look a little different.

Most payroll services impound your payroll taxes with each payroll, so if you use a payroll service, the balance of this account will usually be zero. If you pay your own taxes, there will be a balance in this account until you pay the applicable taxes when they are due.

It is critical not to spend any of this money on anything else! It is *not* your money and spending it instead of sending it to the government can land you in jail. By putting all of the taxes in the payroll account with each payroll, you will eliminate the temptation of spending the money. If there is a balance in the account, you need to make sure that the taxes have in fact been paid. Think of it as a second checkpoint.

Profit First doesn't work without the bank accounts, so you must have the right solution. You need the bank accounts to provide the structure for the transfers, and the transfers (discussed below) are how you improve your profit. Fortunately, Mike and his team have created a solution. They have partnered with Relayfi.com (lets.bankwithrelay.com/coregroup/) to provide bank accounts designed for Profit First. Relayfi is a non-bank financial tool that allows you to set up to twenty bank accounts for zero monthly fees. They also automate your transfers with percentage amounts, which is a huge help. (Full disclosure: Profit First and the author are affiliates of Relayfi and may receive compensation from them for referring you to them.)

Special Use Bank Accounts

There are several other reasons why you might want to use additional bank accounts. These are not required and may never apply to you. You may use them for a season, or not at all.

1. Vault (Working Capital)

Working capital is a fancy accounting word for reserves for running your business. We will talk about exactly how to prioritize and use profit later, but one of the options is to set up a reserve account for a rainy day.

The need for extra money comes in all different ways such as an unexpected illness or natural disasters. Many of them you cannot control. I mean, can anyone say pandemic? Believe it or not, there were many small businesses during the recent pandemic that had plenty of cash, and the government largesse (e.g., Payroll Protection Program loans) was just gravy to them. Since Profit First businesses had their Vault, they didn't need government help to stay in business.

To be prepared for the unexpected, I recommend six months' worth of all of your fixed expenses as reserve. For example, if your owner's compensation, taxes, and operating expenses are $10,000 per month, then you should shoot for $60,000 in this account. Three months is often sufficient, so set an initial target of that.

Building a permanent amount of cash reserves is huge. Once that money is in the bank, you can truly focus on longer term things in your business. You no longer have to be reactive, trying to make the next sale, or making sure you have money to pay yourself. Only then can you really evaluate your business; quit focusing on the urgent and focus on the important.

2. Equipment Purchase

Looking at that new high-speed camera? You can allocate a certain amount of your profit to set aside in this account. When the balance hits the purchase price, you buy the equipment for cash.

Depending on your business, this might be a permanent account. Allocating a percentage of your profits to replace old equipment on a regular basis is sound business.

3. Hiring a New Employee

You may never have employees, and that is totally okay. If you decide to hire an employee, you might consider setting up an account to build up a cushion before you do. You certainly don't have to, but some business owners find comfort in having the cash to pay for a new employee set aside for a few months before they hire them.

This eliminates the stress of making the decision and keeps you from trying to get them to be productive right out of the gate. It takes time to hire the right person, and to get them up to speed. This account takes the pressure off. To clarify, this is a different account than the aforementioned payroll. The payroll account is to pay your payroll and taxes. This account is to set aside an amount before you hire them, so that the money is there to pay them. Then you would transfer the amount to the payroll account for each payroll.

4. Growth/Expansion

I can tell you from personal experience that you can grow yourself into trouble. Many of these troubles arise from not having enough money to fund the growth. We will discuss more on that later in Chapter 9, but setting aside a portion of your profits for growth and expansion can be a great help. It keeps you from growing too fast without enough cash.

Now that you have your bank accounts set up, we'll move on to what to do with them.

1. Transfers (Allocations)

The second key component of Profit First is Transfers or Allocations. I use the terms interchangeably. Allocations are how you ensure your business is going to make a profit by transferring your money to the discrete accounts. Different businesses transfer their money on different schedules depending on their needs. If your work is more project based, you may want to do transfers monthly. Some businesses only want to pay bills twice a month, while others want to do it every Friday. There is no *right* answer. What is most important is that you *have* a schedule, and that you keep it. Remember, we're building habits! If you are unsure where to start, do transfers every time you make a deposit. You can always adjust the timing later.

Let's assume that you've decided to do your allocations on the 15th and end of the month. You will take a fixed percentage of the money in the deposit account on the 15th and end of the month and transfer (allocate) to each account: profit, taxes, owner's compensation, and operating expenses (OpEx). We will discuss how to determine the percentages to use in the next chapter.

At the end of each calendar quarter, take the balance in the profit account, and write yourself a check. This is your reward for running a profitable business! Take your family on a vacation, put it toward a down payment on a new house. Whatever your personal desire—it doesn't matter. It's yours. Congratulations!

For Michael, the sports videographer we met earlier, allocations were a game changer. Having predictable profits gave him peace of mind, but it was also something tangible. By transferring the money to the profit account, you are guaranteeing that your business will be profitable.

"I knew Profit First worked with my first quarterly distributions. I'm like, oh, cool I get to go on vacation. You know what I mean? It just gives that little extra reward. As a freelancer, it's typical to be head down, like hustle, hustle. There is a bit of culture that promotes that. I like looking at that profit account and just being, oh, wow, there's a pretty nice cushion that you've accumulated."

If you mostly do project work, it probably makes sense to do transfers with each deposit. If you have a lot of retainer work, then weekly or semi-monthly might make more sense. The point is, it doesn't really matter as long as you're consistent.

A word about implementation of Profit First. *Most* people don't fully implement Profit First. Shhh! Don't tell Mike! Most (80 percent) take pieces of the tool and customize it to their business and situation. Most don't set up the second profit account at a separate bank account (vault account). Some never set up a tax account. Businesses that don't set up all of the bank accounts and do the transfers regularly do so because they don't like the structure. While you may get by with going half-ass in implementing Profit First, you could be setting yourself up for failure. I go in depth by analyzing the reasons people fail at implementing Profit First in Chapter 6. Profit First works 100 percent of the time it is used correctly. Follow the process.

It is important to keep the goal (more profit and organization, less stress) in mind. Prioritize profit and have financial clarity around your business. Working with a Profit First Professional will make sure you have a method tailored to your business goals, and I highly recommend not doing it alone!

One more thought on bank accounts and transfers. Using separate accounts and making transfers on a regular basis is creating a new habit. You are prioritizing the money coming in. Profit first, then taxes, next paying yourself, and then you spend the rest. Just going through that process will force you to rethink your business finances.

You might find at the beginning of implementing Profit First that there isn't enough money in the operating account at the end of the month. Well, the first three things (profit, taxes, and yourself) are nonnegotiable, so what are you going to change in your business to make sure you have the money to pay your bills? That is entirely different from putting all of the money in one account and hoping that there is some left over to pay yourself!

2. Establish A Rhythm

In his book *Atomic Habits*, James Clear talks about how habits are formed from learned experiences. Habits are formed of four distinct elements: cue, craving, response, reward. If we consistently receive a reward from learned experiences, we will form a habit around them. The reward in this case is more profit! But you have to change your habits first.

Your cue will be when you make a deposit into your bank. Your immediate craving might be to spend it on new software or equipment. But rather than acting on that craving, the response will be to transfer a portion of the deposit into your profit account. Because this money isn't in your OpEx account, you can't spend it. Then, once a quarter, you're going to give yourself a portion of that profit as a reward. I'll go into more detail about what to do with your profit in the next chapter.

I recommend that you pay your bills at the same time you do your allocations. You already know how much you transferred, so you know what bills to pay from the operating account. Depending on what you did when you set up your bank accounts, you may need to change all of your automated bank drafts to your operating account (OpEx). Nothing should be coming out of your deposit or profit accounts. The exception to this would be payroll, in which case you will use the payroll account, if you have employees or pay yourself as a W-2 employee.

As you implement Profit First into your business, be patient. Be mindful that it will take time, at least ninety days, to establish this new habit, and it will take effort. But once you've gone through the cycle of reward, this rhythm will become a habit. At that point, you won't think about habits, they will just happen! Imagine creating a new habit around profit! What is that going to look like for you?

Summary

In this chapter, we learned the key principles that underlie Profit First: Use Small Plates (you can't spend it if it isn't in your OpEx account), Serve Sequentially (you transfer money first to profit, then taxes, then your owner's compensation), and Remove Temptation (by moving the money to a separate account, it is out of sight, out of mind. The mechanics are simple:

- Set up bank accounts.
- Deposit money into your deposit account.
- Move money on a schedule.
- Pay bills from your operating expense account.
- Pay yourself your quarterly profit.

This is the basic Profit First process, and it is simple. Establishing the priority of paying yourself first and establishing new habits is what takes effort.

In the next chapter, we will talk about how to use Profit First to start making more profit.

Chapter 3:
Using Profit First to Increase Profit

For the rest of the book, our focus is going to be on increasing profit so that you can be more creative. In this chapter, I'm going to introduce you to some additional components of Profit First. We will conclude with options for how to use your new profit. This is going to be exciting! I'm not going to lie. There is a special thrill in watching that profit account grow larger. Maybe for me it was because I spent so much of my business life scrambling to have enough cash. I had started out on a quest to help businesses with their finances, but for so long, I didn't do it for myself. I was so focused on growing the business, but I didn't make enough money. Spoiler alert, you can do both, but I used growth as an excuse to not make the profit I should have.

Once you have money in the profit account, you start to view expenditures in a different light. You really do ask yourself, "Do I need to spend that money now, or could it wait, or maybe not be spent at all?"

So, where should you be at this point? Ideally, you've set up your bank account, and you've started your allocations/transfers. You're putting 1 percent of each deposit into your profit account. If you haven't done this yet, *stop*. You need these foundations (bank accounts and transfers) in order to proceed.

Now that you have the tool in place, it's time to decide what you want to build. This process of increasing profit is iterative. You're going to set a goal, and when you achieve it, you may want to set higher goals. These goals should be in line with what you want from your business. Remember, the business should serve your needs. Right now, maybe your goals are simply to fund your personal lifestyle and have predictable profit. That's a great start. After you've achieved that, you may want to take it to the next level, grow, and be even more profitable.

We will do this using three new tools:

- Instant Profit Assessment to give us our Current Allocation Percentages (CAPs)
- Target Allocation Percentages (TAPs)
- Quarterly Implementation Plan

Instant Profit Assessment

> Download Instant Profit Assessment tool at
> www.profitfirst4creatives.com/resources

The first step is to make an honest assessment of where you are and what you have. Profit First calls this the Instant Profit Assessment. You will need some historical financial information to complete this. Ideally, this will take the form of income statements (otherwise known as profit and loss statements) you or your accountant have prepared. If all you have is bank records, and no financial statements, that's fine. You can also use copies of previous business tax returns.

The more data, the better. To get the best picture, I recommend having three years' worth of information, but don't get hung up on the amount you have. This is only giving you a starting place.

Once you have all of the profit and loss information, you will combine them into the categories below for however long you have the information. Combine? Yes, because we are working with percentages. So if you have one year's information, then that is what you will use. If you have three months' worth of data, that is what you will use. If you have three years, you will add them together and use the totals.

If you're using tax returns, you will find the information on Schedule C of Form 1040 (if you are filing as a sole proprietor). Otherwise, the information will be on the first page of Form 1120, 1120S, or 1065.

Using the Instant Profit Assessment tool, we will compute our Current Allocation Percentages or CAPs. These percentages tell you where your business is now; it's really that simple. You're going to have a CAP for taxes, payroll-owner, payroll-employees (if applicable), operating expenses, and profit. These percentages will tell you, for instance, how much profit as a percentage of your real revenue that your business has made in the past. Knowing where you are is foundational to goal setting. You don't set a weight loss goal without first stepping on the scale to see how much you weigh, right?

The Instant Profit Assessment will determine what your Current Allocation Percentages are. We have a simple spreadsheet available for free along with a bunch of other great stuff at www.profitfirst4 creatives.com/resources you can download if you prefer, or you can open up the old Google Sheets and recreate. This is what you want it to look like:

INSTANT PROFIT ASSESSMENT TEMPLATE

PROFIT ASSESSMENT	AMOUNT	CAP	ADJUST	TAP
REAL REVENUE				
TAXES				
PAYROLL - OWNER				
PAYROLL - EMPLOYEES				
OPERATING EXPENSES				
PROFIT				
TOTALS				

Some definitions are in order.

Real Revenue: This is the income you receive *less* any amounts you have to pay subcontractors. For many of you, this will not be applicable. In that case your real revenue will simply be your revenue, the amount you deposited in the bank.

For example, say you have a $10,000 job but need to hire staff for a remote shoot location that costs you $2,000. Your real revenue will be $8,000. The reason that we say your *real revenue* is $8,000 is that we want to 1) standardize our information for comparison to others (we go over this in Chapter 5), and 2) eliminate money that isn't really ours—it is owed to someone else, so we don't want to include it.

To calculate your real revenue, you may have to do some digging if you don't have a good bookkeeping process (See Chapter 7). If you don't have good records, you can use estimates for this exercise. Remember, this is a starting point, your "weigh-in." Precision isn't critical to your success.

Taxes: If your company paid anything for your personal income taxes, include that amount here. This is not for other taxes (e.g., sales tax).

Payroll-Owner: Regardless of how you take money from the company (W-2, or distributions), include the amount here. If you do pay yourself a W-2 wage, include all of the employer taxes here as well (e.g., FICA).

Payroll-Employees: If you have employees, put all of their related expenses here. Include your employer taxes (e.g., FICA) as well as any benefits you might pay for them. Don't forget to include the amount for workers' compensation insurance. The idea here is that we have the *total* cost of employees in this amount.

Operating Expenses: Essentially all other business expenses that aren't in the above amounts.

Profit: This is the total of your revenue less all of the lines for expenses above. You can either use a formula or manually calculate.

Totals: For the totals line, simply use the sum formula to total all of the lines except real revenue. This amount should equal your real revenue and is a double check to make sure you've entered the amounts correctly.

The easiest way to compute your CAPs is to use a spreadsheet. I realize some of you may be spreadsheet challenged but if you stick with me you won't end up frustrated. I'll guide you, and if you have trouble, please email me at profitfirst@coregroupus.com.

First, you're going to put in the totals for however long you have financial information into the Amount column. You do this in column B. Because we're calculating percentages, it doesn't matter if the total is for three months or three years. Remember, the longer the time period of data you've gathered, the better the assessment.

Now, move to the CAP column (C) to enter your formulas. For each line, we're going to compute the percentage of that item by the Real Revenue, by dividing the amount column. For example, the CAP for Payroll-Owner is B3 divided by B1 or C3=B3/B1. You will continue this for each line.

You should end up with something like this:

INSTANT PROFIT ASSESSMENT

A	B : AMOUNT	C : CAP	D : ADJUST	E : TAP
• REAL REVENUE	$100,000			
• TAXES	0	0		0
• PAYROLL - OWNER	20,000	20%		20%
• PAYROLL - EMPLOYEES	40,000	40%		40%
• OPERATING EXPENSES	20,000	20%	(1%)	19%
• PROFIT	20,000	20%	1%	21%
• TOTALS	$100,000	100%		100%

In this example, using the numbers provided, we're going to start by targeting an increase of 1 percent in profit. We use 1 percent because it is a small change that can be relatively easy to implement. We'll discuss this more below in how to determine your Target Allocation Percentages.

Of course, the math says it has to come from somewhere, so we're going to say it's coming from operating expenses. We make a reduction in operating expenses because we don't want to lower what you are paying yourself (Payroll-Owner) or taxes. Remember the order of priority of your allocations: profit, taxes, owner pay. I suppose you could make a reduction in your payroll for employees, but that would probably be more difficult than cutting 1 percent from your other operating expenses.

How to Determine Your Target Allocation Percentages (TAP)

Another key component of Profit First is Target Allocation Percentages or TAPs. TAPs indicate where you want to go, your goal. If your CAPs are your weigh-in, your starting point, TAPs are your goal weight. As in a weight loss goal, your TAPs are very personal to you. I would recommend setting TAPs modestly. Maybe your initial TAPs just cover your personal living expenses. As with many goals, once you achieve your initial goal, you want to push further. Start with TAPs that you can achieve over the next twelve to eighteen months.

If you want to take your goals higher, you will have some information regarding your industry to compare. We give you some benchmarks for comparison to consider in Chapter 5 and discuss why you may want to make a comparison to your peers. Not that you want to be like everyone else, but it gives you an idea of what is possible. If they can make that much money, so can you!

Quarterly Implementation Plan

Download the Quarterly Implementation Plan at www.profitfirst4creatives.com/resources

Once you've determined what your TAPs are, you can create a Quarterly Implementation Plan. A sample is available on our website (www.profitfirst4creatives.com/resources). A Quarterly Implementation

Plan breaks the end goal down into bite-size chunks. To continue the weight loss comparison, you're likely not going to lose all the weight you want to in the first month. The Quarterly Implementation Plan sets interim goals of ninety days. It will look something like this:

QUARTERLY IMPLEMENTATION PLAN

SUBJECT	ACTUAL	Q1	Q2	Q3	Q4	Q5	Q6
• PROFIT ALLOCATION ADJUSTMENT	0	2	3	3	2	3	2
• PROFIT ALLOCATION CUMULATIVE	0	2	5	8	10	13	15
• OWNER'S PAY ALLOCATION ADJUSTMENT	0	2	1	2	2	1	2
• OWNER'S PAY ALLOCATION CUMULATIVE	10	12	13	15	17	18	20
• TAX ALLOCATION ADJUSTMENT	0	2	2	2	2	2	2
• TAX ALLOCATION CUMULATIVE	3	5	7	9	11	13	15
• OPEX ALLOCATION ADJUSTMENT	0	-6	-6	-7	-6	-6	-6
• OPEX ALLOCATION CUMULATIVE	87	81	75	68	62	56	50

Again, I would stick to the twelve-to-eighteen-month timeline here. If yours is only for two or four quarters, that is totally fine. The key is to make progress each quarter, so the bigger the difference between your CAPs and TAPs, the longer your plan will be. You will put the TAPs you computed in the last column (in this example eighteen months from now) and work back to your left to set your interim, quarterly goals.

In the above chart, we want to move from a CAP of zero profit (Actual column) to a profit of 15 percent. We do this by adjusting our profit TAP by two to three percentage points each quarter (the first line). When doing your allocations/transfers throughout the quarter, you will be using the cumulative lines. The adjustment lines show the change for the quarter.

To summarize so far, we've done our Instant Profit Assessment to determine our Current Allocation Percentages (CAPs). We've decided on our long-term profit goal and broken it down into manageable changes by quarter with the Quarterly Implementation Plan. Now we'll discuss how to actually implement the plan.

Getting from CAP to TAP

You have your Quarterly Implementation Plan, now what? The key to improving profitability is to set reasonable expectations. Early gains can come quickly, but reaching your ultimate goal will take time. As Michalowicz says, you don't go from lying on the couch to running a marathon. You're going to hurt yourself if you do. You start with a program that builds you to a 5k, or by walking.

To increase profit, we start by setting modest goals by quarter. Maybe your goal is to improve your profit from 20 to 22 percent. That may seem modest, but it is actually a 10 percent increase in profitability! If you increase by 10 percent every quarter, you'll be at 30 percent in a year and a half. That is no small achievement!

You will reach a point where your increases are going to require more difficult business decisions. For example, you may have to decide that you need to reduce your workforce and fire an employee. Or you may have to reduce your workspace to cut expenses. These challenging decisions can take several months to fully implement.

For example, one of ours took over a year to complete. Our business, Core Group, had way too much space in our building (and this was before everyone was working remotely). At one point we had twenty-five people in our company. We had made the decision to shrink the company (more on that in Chapter 9), and we just didn't need the amount of space we originally had. The other owners and I had discussed it for several years, but Profit First gave us the structure to actually do something about reducing our office space and decreasing our expenses. Because we had allocated a fixed percentage to profit, we had to reduce our operating expenses. Rent was by far our largest non-employee expense, so it had to be lowered somehow.

To complicate matters, the owners of Core were not the same owners of the company that owned the real estate. I owned the company that owned the real estate, while my two partners didn't. When discussing Core's rent expense, my feeling was that I was just paying myself the rent, so reducing the rent really didn't matter to me. I was just moving money from one pocket to another.

But because we were committed to Profit First, we moved into one-half of the building and renovated the building to allow for a second tenant. This allowed Core to cut rent in half. Now you may say, yeah but you spent a bunch of money to renovate the building. Yes, but remember, we were implementing Profit First in Core. We had to consider the company that owned the building (me) separately. If we had a third-party landlord, we would have cut our space when the lease was up and reduced our expenses.

The above example is one of the difficult decisions, but don't start there. When your TAPs say that you need to reduce operating expenses by 1 percent for the quarter, there are probably several expenses that you could cut to get there. Go for the low hanging fruit first. Get some easy wins under your belt. By doing so, by proving your capabilities to yourself, you will have the confidence to tackle the bigger changes. Again, don't overexert yourself. Just as when you train for a marathon, this takes time.

Next, we'll discuss how to prioritize the profit you've earned through implementing your Quarterly Improvement Plan.

What to Do with Profit

As I'm sure you know, it is your company and your profit, so you can arguably do whatever you want with it. However, if you want to thrive and be profitable, I recommend that you focus on using your profit on these items in this order as this will ensure you obtain your desired quality of living, which will in turn give you the motivation and the resources financially, mentally, and emotionally to fund your business. These items are in this order to ensure you have the foundation to move from one step to the other. If you don't have enough profit to fund your lifestyle, there is no reason to move forward and allocate your profit toward funding your Vault.

1. Lifestyle

Obviously, your business serves you (or at least it should), so your first priority should be paying yourself. Assuming that you read the first chapter on mindset, and have your personal financial house in order, build your profit to where you need it personally.

Your business funds your lifestyle, but at what cost of time to you? Your business may make enough profit to fund your life, but are you having to work sixty or eighty hours a week? If so, you may consider using your profit to hire an employee and delegate low value activities to give you more time.

The best way I can explain is the way it was explained to me. I was considering whether to hire someone in our company to prepare tax returns. My colleague asked me what that person would cost. I said, maybe $50,000 a year. He said if I don't hire this person, I'm working for $50,000. That was a revelation to me. For you, it may be hiring someone to do postproduction editing for $50,000, but now you have twenty-five hours of your time back. Yes, it probably takes someone thirty-five hours to do what you can do in twenty-five, but it may be worth it.

Certainly, do what you *want* to do in the business, but if you can hire and delegate, you have more time. There is no substitute for that. Your priority is funding your life *and* not working any more than you want to.

2. The Vault

After your business is consistently producing profit to fund your lifestyle (both profit *and* time), it's time to fund your Vault account discussed in Chapter 2. You may be tempted to focus on something else first, like debt repayment, but trust me; once that vault is full, your business and your life change. Having three to six months of expenses in the bank relieves a lot of pressure, and allows you to be even more proactive, instead of reactive, in your business decisions.

3. Equipment Purchase

Next, consider what you want and need for your business. Recall that we discussed why you have to be careful when purchasing equipment. We can't be the kids in the candy store (no matter how much we'd like to be—nor should we be, even *if* we have the money). Of course, neither do we want to starve the business.

The reason I place purchasing new equipment or any other large ticket item (e.g., software) after funding your Vault is to lay the foundation for success. You may think you need new equipment, but can you get by for another year with what you have? Your business will need upgrades to remain efficient and competitive. Make sure you have a plan to fund it. And by plan, I mean that you have a crystal-clear idea of how the expenditure is going to make more profit. I will discuss this in more detail in Chapter 6. You can use cash or debt, whichever you are comfortable with.

4. Capital for Growth

I go into more depth on growth in Chapter 9 in the Stages of Growth Section, where I discuss the things needed to grow your company at each stage. Money (capital) is just one of the problems you must solve to grow. But let's assume that you do want to grow your business. Most creative businesses don't require a lot of money to fund their growth, but there will be pinch points you will need to fund.

The first pinch point will be your first employee. There will come a time when you have to have help in order to take on more. Many creatives never get to that point, and that is totally fine, as this isn't applicable to every business. However, if you do want to grow by hiring an employee, review our discussion earlier on the subject in Chapter 3, and assess if you need or want a cash reserve before you hire that person.

The second pinch point will likely be space. Maybe you want to rent a space with a studio. Even if you rent a space, this is likely going to be a big jump in your operating expenses. Of course, you're not going to rent the space if it doesn't make you more profit. Increasing profit will take some time after adding that expense. Consider having a reserve saved to offset the increased expense before you make the jump. This will give you the freedom to go and increase your profit rather than worry about paying rent.

A third pinch point might be adding a service offering. Maybe you decide to bring editing back in-house rather than sub it out. This might involve an additional employee, additional equipment and software, or likely both. Again, having the funding set aside before you make those changes will give you breathing room to do it right without the stress.

5. Debt Reduction

The Dave Ramseys of the world have given debt a bad name and to be sure, on many forefronts, being a debt-free, low-risk investor and entrepreneur yields a lot of security, but it's not necessarily conducive for facilitating growth. For those familiar with Dave Ramsey, recall that in his guidance, he is almost exclusively talking about personal finance. One thing entrepreneurs need to learn is that some personal finance principles don't translate for business finance, and the use of debt is one of such principles.

Using profit to eliminate debt *can* be a very good thing. But all debt is not equal, and you don't want to use your profit to reduce debt that causes new problems. Let's look at debt in more detail, including the following:

- Good Debt/Bad Debt
- Eliminating Debt
- Effect on Cash Flow
- Tax Consequences
- Risk

1. Good Debt/Bad Debt

What you need to know about debt is there's good debt and bad debt. Bad debt is debt that costs you money. Good debt makes you money. Yes, all loans charge interest, but does the money you borrow increase profit, net of the interest costs? Bad debt doesn't.

Examples of bad debt usually come from an unprofitable business. Borrowing money on a credit card to keep the lights on is a sign of an unprofitable business. You shouldn't keep borrowing money to keep an unprofitable business going. Either fix the profit problem or shut it down. The worst-case scenario is to keep borrowing until you can't borrow any more, the business shuts down, and you're left with a bunch of debt. That's the kind of debt that you'll probably have to pay back personally, and with no business from which to pay it.

Many creatives who do project work have a cash flow problem that can lead to a profit problem. They receive money in big, sporadic chunks and because they don't use Profit First, they don't properly allocate their money, and inadvertently spend their profit. Then when there is a month with no work, they borrow money until the next project. Using Profit First properly, they will have money set aside for those down months (see Vault/Working Capital in Chapter 2).

Good debt, on the other hand, allows you to seize opportunities that make you more profit. An example would be a high-speed camera that costs $200,000. It would take you a lot of time to save enough profit (and taxes) to pay cash for that. Yes, there is additional risk with debt. You need to be sure that the decision is a *good* business decision and not a function of shiny object syndrome.

Another example of a case of good debt is real estate. There are many reasons you might want to purchase a space separate from your home, like an office or warehouse building. Often times you can subsidize your own space by renting part of the real estate to others. Additionally, there are some significant tax benefits to owning your own business real estate. Obviously, you're probably not going to be able to save enough profit to purchase a building with cash. For most businesses, the purchase of your own space is a relatively low-risk way to build wealth outside of your business, just like buying your home instead of renting it.

2. Eliminating Debt

Given that, one of the best uses of your profit is to eliminate unnecessary debt, when you get to your quarterly profit distribution, you can take part of that and make an extra principal payment on your loan. I recommend taking the loan with the biggest impact on cash flow and paying that off first. You could pick the one with the highest interest rate, but the reduced interest expense is usually negligible after tax.

So which loan has the biggest cash flow impact? I would look at two things, payment amount and term of the loan. There's the simple method and the advanced method.

- Simple method: Usually, you want to take the item with the *lowest* balance and pay it off first. This frees up that payment amount to apply to your next lowest loan balance. This is the proverbial snowball method. As you eliminate loans, you take the payment amount of that loan and apply it to debt reduction. This has a snowball effect as you pay off loans.
- Advanced method: The exception to the simple method I add is to look at the term of the loan. If you have a longer-term equipment loan (say five years), it may make more sense to pay that one off last. In a traditional business finance situation, you want to match your liabilities with your assets.

In achieving this, you should start with paying off your unsecured loans, such as a line of credit or credit cards. Once you have a zero balance on these, you can move on to your secured loans, which are usually longer term. Secured loans are ones where the lender has a "security interest" in property you own. The most common example is equipment loans. When a bank loans you money to purchase equipment, that loan is "secured" by taking the equipment as collateral. If you don't pay back the loan, the lender can repossess the collateral (i.e., the equipment) and sell it to repay the loan. Another common example of a secured loan is your car loan.

We pay off unsecured loans first to avoid having a lot of working capital loans at the same time that you have long-term assets (e.g., equipment, real estate) that are not financed. I've seen this most often when people use a line of credit or credit cards to purchase equipment. It is better to keep lines of credit and credit cards available for working capital and obtain a separate loan for long-term assets such as equipment.

3. Effect on Cash Flow

When talking about paying off debt, it is important to match your debt term to the life of the underlying asset. For instance, if a piece of equipment is going to be obsolete in three years because of technology, then you don't want to finance it for five. Likewise, you don't necessarily want to have to pay off a building in five years. Now, you may *choose* to do that with your profits, and that's fine, but a building is going to be around after five years.

Working capital loans, such as lines of credit or credit cards, are short term, meaning within one year. There should be no balance carrying over year after year. If you are carrying balances on these items, consider using your profit to reduce your debt over time.

One financial ratio we use to advise clients is the coverage ratio. This is the amount of cash flow the company generates divided by the amount of the loan payments. The higher the ratio the better. An example:

Annual Net Income (profit):	$100,000
Total Loan Payments for the year:	$25,000
Coverage Ratio	4:1

For creatives, you want a ratio of 4:1 or higher. This means that if something should happen to cash flow and profit, you are still able to make your loan payments. If your ratio is below four to one, then you need to 1) increase profit and/or 2) eliminate debt. If you don't have the profit, it is unlikely that you will have extra cash laying around to pay off debt. In that case, you can consider refinancing your loans over a longer period. This may or not be an option depending on several factors, such as your total debt, collateral, credit history, and most importantly, profitability.

4. Tax Implications

Another aspect of debt to consider pertains to taxes. There are two components of debt that affect taxes: principal and interest. The first is the principal of the loan: the amount you borrow. Borrowing and repaying money are not counted for taxes. However, when you purchase equipment with that loan you can write off that equipment for taxes.

Most of the time with equipment you can write it off on your taxes very quickly, usually in the year you purchase it. This is great, except that you don't get any more write-offs in the subsequent year. If you borrowed money to finance the equipment, you are in a situation where you have cash going out repaying the loan, but you have no tax benefit from it. This is generally not a situation you want to be in, because you have cash going out the door for which you will not have a tax benefit, and you will owe tax on those amounts.

Using Profit First and working with a Profit First Professional, this situation won't be a problem, since the amount you are allocating to your tax account should provide for this. If you are doing Profit First yourself, understand those loan payments coming out of your OpEx account are not necessarily going to be deductible for income taxes. You may be wondering why. However, there's a lot more to this, and we will cover tax strategies in greater depth later in Chapter 8.

The second component of debt is interest. Interest is deductible for income tax purposes. When evaluating whether or not you are going to borrow money, consider using the after-tax interest cost. Because you receive a tax deduction for the interest, you're actually paying a lower rate on that interest.

To arrive at your after-tax interest cost simply multiply the interest rate of the loan by one minus your tax rate. For example, if your tax rate is 25 percent and the interest rate on the loan is 8 percent, then your after-tax interest rate is .08 * (1-.25) = .06. So, the 8 percent loan only costs you 6 percent after you receive the benefit of deducting the interest on your taxes.

Risk

The last topic in this debt umbrella we are going to cover is risk. Financial companies use the term *leverage* when discussing a company's debt risk. For creatives, this generally isn't a problem, but it is still something to consider. Financial leverage is expressed as a debt ratio, or the total of your debt divided by the equity in your business. Equity is the difference between your assets and your liabilities. The higher your ratio, the more risk your business has.

The debt ratio for a creative business should be below 1:1. Here's an example.

Assets (cash, equipment)	$200,000
Less: Liabilities (bank loan)	$100,000
Equals: Equity	$100,000
Leverage Ratio (liabilities divided by equity)	1:1

Lenders can cause you a lot of hassle, and even force you into bankruptcy. You want to make sure that if you are using debt to grow your business, you are giving yourself enough slack to avoid this. Maintaining a leverage ratio below 1:1 and a coverage ratio above 4:1 will keep you out of long-term trouble. As I said, I'm not opposed to debt, but it is an obligation. Whether you can comfortably pay for it or not, it's there. Consider eliminating debt and that future obligation on your business as your next step.

Summary

At the beginning of the chapter, we talked about Current Allocation Percentages (CAPs), and doing an Instant Profit Assessment to compute yours. We talked about setting up Target Allocation Percentages (TAPs) to establish your profit goals, and then showed how to use a Quarterly Implementation Plan to get there.

We also discussed how to prioritize what to do with the profit, once you made it. The suggested order of priority starts with funding your lifestyle, and then funding your Vault. We also talked about using profit for the elimination of debt, and why debt isn't necessarily a bad thing, and the various issues surrounding debt.

Before we move on to the next chapter, let's summarize what you need to do:

- Do an Instant Profit Assessment to determine where you are financially (www.profitfirst4creatives.com/resources).

- Establish your TAPs for the next quarter (www.profitfirst4creatives.com/resources).
- Start using those TAPs each time you transfer money from your deposit account.
- Determine what you want to use your profit for.

Eventually, you are going to run out of expenses to cut, and where do you go from there? We will discuss the most powerful profit improvement tool in the next chapter.

Chapter 4:
Unlock Your Value with Pricing

Pricing seems to be a mystery to many business owners, and with good reason. It is not an exact science. Most accountants advise their clients on pricing by starting with costs. Although it makes sense to start with what your costs are and determine your pricing based upon them plus some amount of expected profit, it leaves a lot of potential money on the table. An alternative method is Value Pricing, where you focus on the value you deliver, and the value the customer perceives. For many of you this will be completely new, and life changing!

Several years ago, we were doing some project work for a client. I had recently been introduced to the concept of Value Pricing, and I wanted to try it out. My brother was actually working with the client, and I asked him to give Value Pricing a try. I asked him how much time he had on the project, and he replied maybe five hours.

I knew that the client received tremendous value for what we did, so I asked my brother, what is the most you would charge him. He responded that maybe $2,500, thinking that charging $500 an hour was awesome. I suggested to try letting the client determine the pricing. Simply show him the value you created for him and let him decide what he wants to pay.

The client came back and paid us $20,000! That is the power of changing your thinking about pricing from time and cost to what value the customer perceives. I don't recommend this specific method of letting the customer decide at the end of the project what to pay. This application of value pricing really only works with transactional services, in our case tax consulting, but the principle of pricing for value is applicable in all products and services.

In this chapter, we will define what Value Pricing is and how to implement it in your business, along with several real-world examples of creatives doing it in their businesses. Last, we'll define and discuss the Pareto Principle and how you can use it to further enhance your personal value.

Value Pricing

By far the most powerful leverage for profit in your business is what you charge. Hands down. In fact, I will bet you that changes in pricing will have a bigger impact on your bottom line than all of the other changes you make combined. There are three components to Value Pricing:

- Problem
- Solution
- Unique Value Proposition

Almost everyone in business, especially creatives, underestimates their value and prices accordingly. This makes sense if you're just starting, not sure what you should charge, and are just surviving. It is not a strategy for profitability.

Most businesses start out with a service or product in mind. They think they can do it better or see additional demand and they start. Their pricing follows the market, what everyone else is charging. Over time, they refine their service offering and pricing based upon what they uniquely provide. But this actually skips a critical step in pricing.

Think about starting your company over from scratch. I recommend an awesome tool from leanstack.com called a Lean Canvas (www.profit4creatives.com/resources). This was developed for the technology space for startups, but it works in any business. It is essentially a one-page business plan. The parts I want to focus on are the parts about the customer. This is not a part of Profit First and is applicable to your business whether you implement Profit First or not.

My first Canvas   Mar 26, 2021

PROBLEM	SOLUTION	UNIQUE VALUE PROPOSITION	UNFAIR ADVANTAGE	CUSTOMER SEGMENTS
O/E doesn't know how to diagnose cause of their pain	Assessment to determine underlying cause	No more guessing about what the problem is and whether solution will fix the problem	Curated list. Assuming that most other website directories are pay-to-play and they list any service provider so as to earn more revenue on listings	Owners and execs whose #growth is not meeting expectations
O/E doesn't know how to source & evaluate available external resources	Curated service providers to solve cause	Curated list of service providers – not just a paid listing service		Owners and execs whose business is in crisis
When O/E engages more than one consultant/service provider often these outside contractors don't have access to information about what the other is doing or prescribing, and this can lead to O/E and business getting conflict help	Online platform where service providers and client can access and share data and strategy documents and plans to ensure alignment across all players and strategies	Unique data room where confidential information can be shared by the user to all their consultants/service providers	Unique data room where consultants can communicate and collaborate to provide the best overall results for the client	Owners and executives looking for personal leadership coaching
			Unique AI dative assessment questionnaire perhaps backed up by humans who make a refined assessment following the initial diagnosis by online questionnaire	Owners and executives looking for #strategic planning consulting
				Owners and execs whose profitability is not meeting expectations

This is a sample of an actual idea I had a couple of years ago. I started at the left with the problem and moved to the right. To be honest, this idea never went anywhere, so it might not be the best example, but it will work for our purposes.

1. Problem

Start by defining the problem, *as the client/customer* sees it. Use their language, not yours. This is actually pretty difficult for existing businesses because you will want to use words that you are already using internally, or worse, your existing marketing language. To proceed and be successful, you have to write it as your customer says it. For example, for my business, they want simplified, organized finances with no surprises. They want a guide who can talk to them in terms they understand.

2. Solution

Again, define your solution in terms the customer would understand. Here your existing marketing copy might be helpful, but maybe not. The point is the solution has to be clear and simple for the customer to understand. No technical details! Our solution example is *we provide a responsive, helpful guide to have clarity around your finances and a straightforward process to manage them.*

3. Unique Value Proposition

You may have heard of this term before. It should flow naturally from your solution language. It defines your solution as a value statement and should be a removal of the problem. This statement should be self-evident and transformative. It shouldn't need additional explanation.

While drafting this book, I was prompted to create a core message, which is a very similar concept. You may or may not recall already reading it, in the first chapter. Just in case, here it is again:

> **You don't have to compromise your creativity to make a profit. Creativity and profitability are complementary!**

In a very real way, that is the Unique Value Proposition of this book.

Here are John Jantsch's thoughts on what this looks like for creatives.

"I think that it's (referring to my core message above) going to be the only profitable space left for creatives. I spoke at a conference yesterday, and one of the first speakers was using AI and design, and it was all about, look at this cool stuff it can do.

"Nobody was talking about the strategic aspects that a truly creative person can bring, that no AI will. AI doesn't think outside the box. **The real value of a creative person is somebody who can package, who can take two things and put them together.** Somebody that's truly creative, and you're like, wow, I never would have thought of that. And it was literally somebody that was paying attention to something that looked truly unique to them, and they were actually able to bring it into the world."

I'm going to pause here before we proceed. Coming up with the first three items for your business is going to be hard. It is going to require you to dive deep into your client's business. You need to have a very clear idea of what their problems are, the pain they cause, and *the cost* associated with them. I'm going to be honest with you, when I work with businesses on their Lean Canvas, many quit simply because it is hard, and it is new to them. Currently, I'm working on my notes from my editor for this book. This is my first book, and I've never done this before, and it is *hard*. Remember discussing the Greek root of the word *passion*, in Chapter 1? You have to have a passion for your business that will get you through this hard stuff. Remember why you are doing this. If you want to add rocket fuel to your pricing and profit, don't quit!

How to Find the Problem/Solution

Start with talking to your clients/customers, a lot. It's a simple task, but it's not easy. Start with questions like, "What problem are you (your client) trying to solve?" Or, "If this problem is solved, what will that do for your (your client's) business?" Having deep dives with your customers will teach you a ton. You may find out that what you are providing is only a partial solution to their overall problem, or you may reveal that they actually have a much bigger problem you didn't even know about.

You're possibly going to look at that problem and say, "Well I can't fix all of that." Good news! You don't have to. Maybe you are only part of the solution and have to bring other service providers to the table to provide a complete solution. The thing is, when you solve their whole problem, you receive the maximum value (price). Since you know the scope of the problem, you're in the driver's seat. Instead of partnering with other service providers, you run point, and hire subcontractors to do the things you can't.

Once you have the problem, solution, and value nailed down, you can start to think about pricing, but in an entirely different way. If the solution for your client has a value of $100,000, how do you price your solution? Is it based upon your time or costs? Maybe, but if so, you're probably going to leave a lot of money on the table. Alternatively, if you look at your time and cost, you might decide that there is no way to make the amount of profit you need and look for something else.

But assuming that you can solve the problem and can deliver the solution, how do you price it? You start with their best alternative. What other solution is available to them? Maybe they could do it in-house, but at what cost and time? Is there someone else in the market that can deliver the total solution, and if so, what do they charge? Ideally, there won't be any other realistic alternative.

That is when you can charge literally whatever you want, up to the solution value. Obviously, they aren't going to pay $200,000 for something that is worth only $100,000 to them. No. But would they pay $50k? $60k? $70k?

See what happened there? You shifted your entire focus from your costs and time to the value you are delivering. That is *the* essence of pricing for value.

Our Example

Let's take my business as an example. Nominally we provide bookkeeping, tax, payroll, and Profit First consulting services. The first thing you'll notice is that we bundle *all* our services.

We don't offer any of our services stand-alone. They come in packages. We actually came to this arrangement not because we were trying to maximize prices, but because we knew that if we did these services individually for businesses, we weren't completely solving their problem. It's really hard to do taxes correctly if you don't have accurate and timely bookkeeping. In other words, we did it for selfish reasons. Bundling made our job easier.

But let's look at our least expensive service, tax preparation. We created this service offering for those creatives who were just starting out or for those whose business was a side hustle. Those clients don't necessarily need the other services, and often times, they can't afford them.

What are their alternatives? Pricing for tax preparation for businesses is all over the board, from TurboTax to H&R Block among too-numerous-to-count others. You can find someone to prepare your taxes from $150 to $5,000 for our target customer. With such a variety of options, how do you price against that?

Well, to do so, we had to determine what the problem we were solving was. And it wasn't tax preparation. No one knows whether their taxes are done correctly. There is a high level of trust when you hire someone to prepare your taxes. Trust is a table stake. If you don't have that, you're out of the game from the start.

Given that, let's assume that the vast majority of preparers are trustworthy, so now what? We solve two problems for our target beyond just providing a tax return. The first, and most important, is communication. Our target customer hates working with their current provider. They find their tax preparers difficult to reach in a timely manner, and when they do reach them, they don't understand what the hell they're saying.

We invest heavily in soft skills such as communication education, emotional intelligence, and differing communication styles. We don't use terms like depreciation and accrual. We speak so they can understand. More importantly, we listen so that we understand what their real issues and concerns are.

The second problem we solve is eliminating surprises. With every tax return we prepare, we offer a projection for the coming year, and update it with new information throughout the year. By adding the projection to the service offering, the client knows what their tax bill is going to be months in advance of filing their return.

We give them understanding (peace of mind) and eliminate surprises. You think we can price higher than TurboTax and H&R Block now? You bet! We can charge them what they probably are already paying with another accounting firm, but they receive way more value.

Our Client's Example

Let's look at an actual example from one of our clients. Ryan is a seasoned production veteran who works with universities and schools, and this is what he had to say about his journey. Like many of you, when he first began his business, he focused pricing on his time and the client's budget.

"The pricing model we and so many of the other filmmakers that I know used when we started was *What is that other person charging? I can charge that, and a little bit less, and then probably get the work.* You don't want to charge more than people that you look up to because you just don't believe that your work is worth it.

"But then we started asking questions of our clients. In the discovery process, we would ask the following questions: *If this video goes great, how are you going to use it? What is the potential of this campaign using this video? What's the potential revenue that this could generate? How many clients or how many sales calls will this generate? What would make this all worth it for you?*

"And sometimes people have an answer. Other times they haven't really thought that far, they just know that they need video. The follow-up question is this: *Let's say you don't do a video, what kind of impact could this have? Would it have an impact, positive or negative, if you don't do it?*

"We worked with clients and learned the potential value of what the video *could be* for them is essentially millions of dollars. So, while I could do the video for $2- to $3,000 of my time and energy, the clients were telling me that if we did this project and we sold two of these things, there was a potential to be worth $300,000, $500,000, $2,000,000. Then I knew that they were putting a lot of value in this video, in this campaign.

"If this video cost $50,000 to help you make that many dollars, that's a pretty good return on your investment. We find ourselves trying to help the client understand the potential value for a video. If they don't value the video, they're going to think that it should cost $1,500 because they are thinking: *I can do this with my phone.*"

Now, you may be thinking that Ryan is playing at a whole other level, and you'd be right. Because Ryan understands the true problem, and the value the solution provides, he can price entirely differently.

This is work, and it is work that most creatives aren't willing to do. Why? Well, not only do you have to have engaging conversations with your clients, but you also have to ask them difficult questions, questions for which they may not have immediate answers. Keep digging, until you can easily answer the question, "If I solve this problem for you, what is that worth to you?" Even if you don't arrive at the answer initially, you are going to uncover powerful pricing information.

Yet Another Example

Many of you may be stuck in the mindset of comparing yourself and your services with your competitors. Several years ago, I don't recall the speaker, but he was discussing pricing at an event I was attending. He held up a bottle of water and asked the question, "How do you price water?" It is literally the most abundant thing on the planet. Why would anyone pay anything for water? Well, most of the water on Earth is not drinkable, so first it has to be fresh water. Then there is your proximity to that fresh water, so obviously there is the benefit of being able to turn on the tap and obtain it when you want or need it.

According to the website Statista, the highest cost of tap water in 2021 was just over two cents a gallon. In 2021, the average price of bottled water was $7.87 per gallon according to the International Bottled Water Association. Can you explain that? I can't. Do I drink bottled water? Yes. Why do I pay that much for something I can get from my kitchen sink? Well, part of my decision is location. I'm at a stadium where you can't bring in beverages.

But that doesn't explain what is going on here. Consider the astounding number of different bottled waters out there and many of them are charging significantly higher prices (e.g., Fiji). What you see is that 1) water price has *nothing* to do with the product's cost and 2) the pricing of the product has everything to do with the value *perceived* by the consumer.

What I want you to see from this example is that value drives potential price, regardless of competitors. If you want to have the market share of Aquafina, then yes, your competition is going to play a role in your pricing, but for the rest of us, it is about finding customers, solving their problem, and extracting the most price we can from the value they receive.

To summarize Value Pricing, you start by clearly identifying the problem as your client/customer understands it. You then determine a novel solution in terms that your client clearly understands. You do this by asking a lot of questions, and understanding the economic impact the complete solution has on the client. Now let's look at how to optimize the delivery of that solution.

Leveraging the Pareto Principle

Once you've defined the Problem/Solution/Value for your client, you have to deliver it. How do you determine what you do versus employees or contractors?

If you are going to turn your passion from a job into a business, you must focus on the 20 percent of your time that produces the most valuable results, and delegate, automate, or eliminate the 80 percent. I'm not suggesting that you are only going to work one day a week; I'm saying you must identify the activities that produce 80 percent of your results and do more of them. These activities will likely evolve over time, as your skills increase and your business changes. Take bookkeeping. Does doing your own bookkeeping produce a lot of value in your business? Maybe, if it is done right, and it certainly must be done. So why are you still doing it? Wouldn't your time be better used creating?

How can I make such a statement? Let's start by going back a couple hundred years. Stick with me. Vilfredo Pareto was a nineteenth century Italian who studied the land ownership in his country. He found that (roughly) 20 percent of the population owned 80 percent of the land. Future economists and intellectuals studied this further and developed the Pareto Principal, which shows up in astonishing ways whenever human activity is involved.

Anyone familiar with the bell curve from school will not be surprised to read this. Most of us learned at an early age that most people are in the middle (earning a grade of C), while a few people earned As, or a few people earn Fs.

PARETO CHART

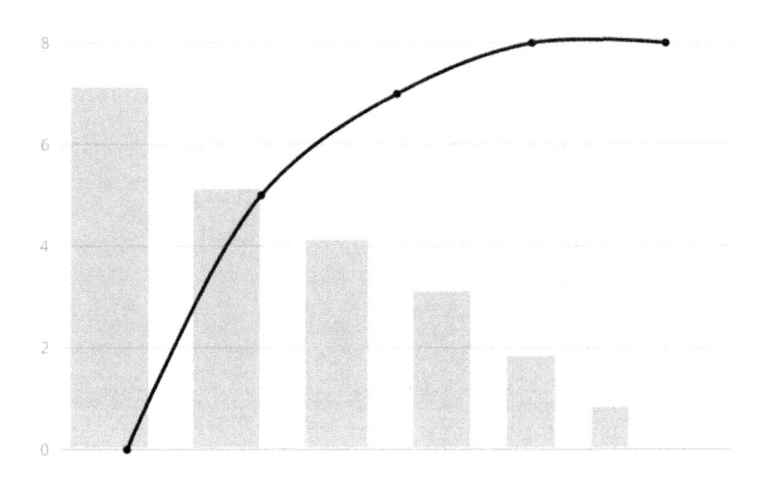

When applying the Pareto Principle to your business, 20 percent of your individual efforts produce 80 percent of your results. Read that again. Put another way, 80 percent of your time is not generally productive. It's work that others can do. Most business owners really struggle with this. They want to control all aspects of the business, which is fine if you don't want to grow. Eventually you're going to have to stop being the bottleneck and allow others to do some of the work. The key here is to use the Pareto Principle to determine what you should delegate to others. You should retain the small percentage (20-30 percent) of the work that produces the most value, and delegate the rest to an employee or contractor.

It also means that a small percentage of people will make the extra effort to improve their business. I'm guessing (if I'm lucky) only 20-40 percent of entrepreneurs in creative industries (our target reader for this book) will ever buy this book, and 20-40 percent of those people will actually read the book. That's 4-16 percent of all creatives will read this book. These are all approximations, but the conclusion is based upon sound human science.

I'll go a step further and tell you that your current customers/clients are willing to spend a lot more money with you using the Pareto Principle. If you have twenty clients paying you $5,000 a year, you're earning $100,000. Using the Pareto Principle, I can estimate that there are four of those that would be willing to pay you an additional $20,000 (an additional $80,000 in revenue) and one of them will pay you $160,000!

How can I estimate this? Well, Pareto says 20 percent of those twenty want more, that's the first four. And 20 percent of those four will pay even more, the one. This is not exact science here, but it does start to show you that if you can provide the solution, your existing clients will pay you more, lots more. But you won't be doing the 80 percent tasks to achieve it. You will have to be dedicating all of your time to those most valuable tasks, the 20 percent.

Eventually you're going to hit the limit of what you can do yourself. It varies, but I see most creatives hitting that level at no more than $350k in revenue. Even if you are satisfied with that level of revenue and profit, wouldn't you like some of your time back?

Nick, our video producer, felt that way. Think back to our discussion in Chapter 1 about the three-prong decision creatives have to make: balancing what customers are willing to pay, what the costs are, and whether the work is creatively satisfying.

"You might have a $50,000 job that your team of internally two people are taking on, but now you're hiring editors, you're getting props for those projects, you're renting gear. And now if you don't budget accordingly, you might have that $50,000 job that's happening in one month, you might be spending $48,000 of it walking away with $2,000, which is just sad if you end up in that position. I think that's the thing if you do it just by yourself.

"On the other hand, you could do all the work, then you then don't realize just how much labor intensive that is. I'm going to do all the editing, I'm going to shoot it, I'm going to produce it, do all of that side. Now you're burned out and you can't take another job. So, it's really hard to find that balance of what you do, and what do you charge? To make it so that way you can actually do the work that you want to do as well as not burn yourself out and still make a profit at the end of the day. It's a fine balance to do all of that."

Say your business is producing commercial videos for businesses. There are a lot of steps involved from pre-production planning to postproduction editing. Which of these are you *really* good at? Which of these drives the real value for your customer?

If you're really good at developing the story and script for the video, hire an employee or contractor to do the postproduction editing to free up your time to do more of the story work.

This is where the owner's compensation and profit come into play. By knowing these percentages and dollar amounts, you can make decisions on what to delegate and what to magnify.

Let's use some hypothetical numbers. Let's say you get paid $25k to produce a commercial for a client. It only takes 20 percent of your time to do the story and script. Let's also assume that you are making 65 percent profit in your business (before taxes and your pay). That means that $25k is going to net you roughly $16k.

Let's also assume that because of time limits, you can only produce ten commercials a year. If you delegated all of the other production activities to employees or contractors, you now are no longer making 65 percent because you have additional costs. BUT you have just freed up 80 percent of your time!

You could use that time to find additional clients and do more commercials. In fact, based upon your time, you could do five times the number (50)! Even with the additional costs and lower profit percentage, you're going to be making more total dollars. *Or*, if you're satisfied with the lower profit, you can do something else with your time—go to the beach!

If I had a dollar for every creative entrepreneur who has conceded profit for the "experience," I would have a lot of dollars. There is a temptation when you have little work product to show a prospective client to concede on pricing. You rationalize that you need the experience to be able to charge more later. This is a perilous wheel to step on because it is inherently self-defeating. One alternative I've seen is to do low-cost work for your favorite charity, and then use that for marketing purposes, including press releases.

Your business must make a profit from the beginning. I'm assuming that you have expertise in your field and can bring value to your customers. Don't be afraid to charge for it, regardless of your so-called lack of experience. The customer is paying for your expertise, not your experience!

There may be times that you will want to price a job low to obtain the business. Usually this is to establish yourself in a new market. Or maybe *you* are trying something new that you're not sure about and want to test it out. If you are going to price a job below your target profit amount, be strategic about it. Be clear about why you are doing it and have an end in mind.

Jon, the Emmy-award-winning sports film producer, not the author, had this to say:

"Sometimes if there's an opportunity that's not super great paying, but it provides an opportunity for me to get a piece for my portfolio that I don't have that will then allow me to get to where I want to go, then I will work with a smaller budget because I have to look at the longer-term picture more than the short term. That's how I got into the sports market: I took a very small, low paying job doing a sports video because I didn't have anything. That helped get me to the next bigger job, and then the next. I've tried to look at some of those opportunities more strategically.

"If I'm going to discount my rates, if I'm going to do this for free, at least it has to have some value for me. If there's a high value to me, and there's enough money to at least cover my hard costs on it, then it's not such a bad deal. Obviously, I can't do that for every project."

Here are my final thoughts on the Pareto Principle. In order to maximize your profit, you have to focus on the creative things you do that provide the most value. All other things should be delegated, automated, or eliminated. You can delegate to employees or contractors or outsource to another partner company.

Summary

In this chapter, we discussed the rocket fuel that is value pricing. By shifting from the pricing method of looking at your cost and adding an expected profit amount to determine your price, you can focus on the perceived or real value received by your customer and price based upon that. We also saw how we can use the Pareto Principle in many aspects of your business, including determining what work is better to delegate to free up you to do more profitable things.

Here are your action items from this chapter:

- Have in-depth conversations with your customers to define their total problem.
- Identify the solution to that problem in terms they understand.
- Determine what that solution is worth to them—their value.
- Revise your pricing to capture the most of that value considering what their alternative solutions are.

In the next chapter, we will discuss how to use the competition to determine what your profit could be.

Chapter 5:
Compare Yourself to Grow Yourself

I remember the first time I compared my financial performance to my peers. I was shocked (I shouldn't have been) by how poorly we did. My first reaction was *that couldn't be right. They don't make that much money.* Then came the rationalizations. *I'm investing in my business!* Yes, in a way I was, but that was still no excuse for not making a proper profit. As it turns out, you can do both, grow *and* invest in your business, while still making a profit.

In this chapter, I want to give you some benchmark information by different types of creative businesses. I'm providing this information only as a reference to let you know what others are doing. I don't present it to put any pressure on you, only to provide a reference point.

This data is combined from our clients and industry information of those who don't use Profit First. They are averages, so most (60 percent) businesses will have these results, while 20 percent will be significantly worse, and 20 percent will be significantly better. We have clients who do not reach these numbers, and that's okay! At the end of the day, Profit First is about creating the business *you* want, not what someone else thinks it should be.

You can also check with other trade groups or other industry resources that will share financial information. We use a service called Bizminer.com, though that is expensive for the individual business owner. They do have a free site, bizstats.com, that you can use that has more limited financial information, including expense amounts and percentages for your industry.

To illustrate, I'm going to present some of the most common creative businesses. If your specific business is not listed, note that I've tried to provide information as to what differs in the profitability of these businesses. Match your business to the one that most closely matches those characteristics.

In using these reference numbers, please review Chapter 3 and how to compute the allocation percentages. Here is a sample so you don't have to flip pages.

INSTANT PROFIT ASSESSMENT

A	B : AMOUNT	C : CAP	D : ADJUST	E : TAP
• REAL REVENUE	$100,000			
• TAXES	0	0		0
• PAYROLL - OWNER	20,000	20%		20%
• PAYROLL - EMPLOYEES	40,000	40%		40%
• OPERATING EXPENSES	20,000	20%	(1%)	19%
• PROFIT	20,000	20%	1%	21%
• TOTALS	$100,000	100%		100%

Also review what is included in each account and pay close attention to the concept of Real Revenue. Remember Real Revenue is your gross income less payments to contractors. If you don't deduct those first, your percentages will not be comparable.

Also, when using Profit First we make the distinction between profit and owner's compensation. When looking at a small business, it is traditional to combine these numbers if you're looking at the profitability of the business. I encourage you to combine these numbers when comparing yourself. This eliminates the confusion of comparing yourself to non-Profit First company data.

Photography

Often times photography is not a stand-alone service. Many people in this space often combine videography with photography (e.g., wedding photographers). These numbers are for pure photography. Without video, you don't have the additional expense of certain software, and postproduction costs are generally lower.

On the flip side, it is difficult to command the same prices with solely providing photography. Photographers usually make up this revenue by selling prints, physically or digitally, with a hefty markup.

Because this service doesn't have many divisible tasks, the business revenue is limited to around $200k per photographer. Scaling beyond that amount requires the owner to hire photographers who are willing to accept less than they can make independently, but who don't want the responsibilities or headaches of business ownership.

PHOTOGRAPHY

REVENUE	UP TO $500K	OVER $500K
• PROFIT	12%	11%
• OWNER'S COMP	17%	18%
• TAX	3%	2%
• OPEX	68%	69%

If you are a photographer, you should be taking home a combined profit and pay of 29 percent in order to be in line with your peers. Photographers average paying between 2-3 percent of their revenue toward their tax bill from their business and spending between 69-29 percent of their total revenue on operating expenses.

Videography

Again, there is a lot of overlap between these services, and we will focus here on pure videographers, including directors of photography.

This service also includes postproduction editing and the final deliverable. For businesses under $500k in revenue, average revenue for videography is usually 50 percent higher than strictly photography companies.

VIDEOGRAPHY

REVENUE	UP TO $500K	OVER $500K
• PROFIT	8%	5%
• OWNER'S COMP	39%	35%
• TAX	0%	1%
• OPEX	53%	59%

Videographers with revenue of less than $500k per year should be netting with profit and owner's compensation 47 percent. So, if you have revenue of $100k, you should be left with $47k after expenses. If you have revenue over $500k, your net profit and compensation will be lower at 40 percent. This is because of increased operating expenses, likely employee expenses. Videographers with over $500k in revenue pay 1 percent of their revenue toward their personal taxes from the business.

Marketing Agencies

It is important to make the distinction between marketing and advertising services. Companies that offer advertising services generally place the ads and charge their clients added agency fees.

MARKETING AGENCIES

REVENUE	UP TO $500K	OVER $500K	ADVERTISING (OVER $500K)
• PROFIT	12%	11%	9%
• OWNER'S COMP	24%	18%	16%
• TAX	3%	2%	0%
• OPEX	61%	69%	75%

Marketing agencies that bill their clients for pass-through advertising costs should be very careful that they are using Real Revenue and net out those advertising costs from their revenue before comparing their percentages. Only include your agency fees on advertising in your revenue number, and use the last column, otherwise your percentages will be incorrect to compare.

Agencies that pass through advertising costs should be netting through profit and owner's compensation 25 percent of their revenue. If you have a $1M revenue agency, you should be netting $250k.

If your agency doesn't pass through advertising costs, your net should be 36 percent if you are under $500k in annual revenue. If your annual revenue is over $500k, your net should be lower at 29 percent, because of increased operating expenses, likely additional employee expenses.

Non-advertising agencies pay on average 2-3 percent of their revenue toward their personal tax bill from the business.

Content Creators/Influencers

At the end of the day content creators and influencers are in the advertising business. Their business model is just slightly different from traditional advertising agencies. And of course, they produce the content!

CONTENT CREATORS | INFLUENCERS

REVENUE	UP TO $500K	OVER $500K
• PROFIT	8%	4%
• OWNER'S COMP	39%	50%
• TAX	0%	8%
• OPEX	53%	33%

Content creators and influencers with under $500k in annual revenue should be netting 47 percent with their profit and owner's compensation. If your revenue is over $500k, that percentage increases to 54 percent. Unlike other industries, content creators and influencers don't generally add employees and other operating expenses as they grow their revenue.

Those content creators with over $500k in annual revenue pay on average 8 percent of their revenue toward their personal tax bill from the company.

Cinematography/Production

The primary distinction here from videography is that there is a production element. Development of the story and vision, pre-production work such as location scouting and set design add to the costs, time, and revenue. Interestingly, the combined profit and owner's compensation remains identical to that of videography alone businesses. Probably because they aren't charging enough!

CINEMATOGRAPHY | PRODUCTION

REVENUE	UP TO $500K	OVER $500K
• PROFIT	3%	10%
• OWNER'S COMP	32%	25%
• TAX	0%	2%
• OPEX	65%	63%

Cinematographers and other production companies with annual revenue under $500k should take home with owner's compensation and profit 34 percent of their revenue. Companies with revenue over $500k in annual revenue should earn slightly more at 35 percent of their revenue.

Cinematographers with annual revenue over $500k pay on average 2 percent of their revenue toward their personal tax bill from the company.

Commercial Art/Graphic Designers

Unfortunately, true designers have the lowest combined profitability and owner's compensation of the group. Hopefully, this book will change that!

COMMERCIAL ART | GRAPHIC DESIGNERS

REVENUE	UP TO $500K	OVER $500K
• PROFIT	6%	2%
• OWNER'S COMP	21%	19%
• TAX	0%	0%
• OPEX	73%	79%

Commercial artists and graphic designers with annual revenue of less than $500k should take home 27 percent of their revenue when combining their profit and owner's compensation. Those with revenue over $500k in annual revenue will only net 21 percent because of the increased operating expenses, likely additional employee costs. Most commercial artists and graphic designers do not pay any of their personal taxes from their businesses.

Interior Design

Interior design is a complicated business combining elements of two different businesses, creative services and construction management. Because many interior designers purchase products for their clients and pass through those costs, the revenues are higher, so I've included an extra segment.

INTERIOR DESIGN

REVENUE	UP TO $500K	$500K TO $1MM	OVER $1MM
• PROFIT	11%	10%	12%
• OWNER'S COMP	16%	16%	21%
• TAX	2%	2%	1%
• OPEX	71%	72%	66%

Interior design companies must pay careful attention to using their Real Revenue when using these percentages for comparison. Do not include pass-through costs and related revenue in your revenue numbers for comparison. If you markup the items, then only include your net profit in those items in your revenue.

For interior design companies with less than $1MM in annual revenue, your business should net (with profit and owner's compensation), between 26-27 percent. If you have revenue over $1MM, you should expect a net of 33 percent. This increase in an owner's take home is because as a percentage of revenue, you won't have as many operating expenses. Interior design is unlike most creative industries in that it scales well, meaning that you don't add a proportionate amount of operating expenses as your revenue grows.

Use your Initial Profit Assessment from Chapter 3 to compare your numbers to these benchmarks. You are looking at long-term goals here. If your benchmark is a 10 percent increase in profit, that is going to take time. Be patient.

Use this information to adjust your Quarterly Implementation Plan. Plan for moderate changes each quarter. The more you must improve, the longer it will take.

Summary

In this chapter, we provided benchmarks by business type to help you compare your business to similar businesses. By comparing our numbers to our peers, we see what profit potential our business has.

Here are your action items from this chapter:

- Take the information you have from your Initial Profit Assessment you did in Chapter 3.
- Compare it to the information in this chapter.
- Decide what you want your long-term goal for your Target Allocation Percentages to be.
- Adjust your Quarterly Implementation Plan accordingly.

In the next chapter, we will discuss the most common problems you will encounter in implementing Profit First and how to overcome them.

Chapter 6:
Common Problems and Solutions

Many entrepreneurs—and creatives especially—struggle with focus. One of the ways this manifests is shiny object syndrome, and I have it, bad. Probably you have it too. In order to properly implement Profit First, you have to find a way to focus on the implementtation and not let the shiny objects distract you. In this chapter, I'll discuss where Profit First implementation falls off the rails, and how to get you back on track. Let's start with my experience with Profit First.

After I heard Mike speak in 2014, I read *Profit First* and then I joined the Profit First Professionals network. The network is a paid membership group of different types of professionals (e.g., accountants, bookkeepers) who help business owners implement and use Profit First. The first requirement of being part of the network was to implement Profit First in our own businesses. At that point in my life, our business finances were awful, and my brother and I were at odds as to how to fix them.

We had three owners and an overly complicated business structure. We had developed this structure over the years because we had multiple owners, and we were trying to accommodate everyone's interests. The structure was also complicated because we had too many services, and some of them required separate ownership. We had three different operating entities, one for each geographic location. Then we had a management company to account for common expenses (e.g., marketing) for the three operating entities. Additionally, we had a separate company to provide public accounting related services, and one to provide our investment services, both of which were required because of licensing.

I think we ended up setting up twenty-five or more bank accounts for the various entities. Because we didn't have enough money, it was a complete disaster moving money back and forth between various companies.

What we did do right was that we ensured the 1 percent of the income went into a separate bank account. We were at the end of the year and were struggling over some financial decision, and my brother said "Well, we've got that money in the profit account." I had completely forgotten about it, which is the way Profit First is supposed to work (i.e., use small plates and remove temptation). And what did I do? I took the money out to spend on whatever it was, which was the *wrong* thing to do. That money was profit not in the operating expense account. I hadn't learned yet to only spend what was in the OpEx account.

But we finally got it right. When the other two owners left, I was able to simplify the business, get rid of all of those extra accounts, and I learned to keep my hands out of the profit account. At the end of the day, the business couldn't afford three owners, and two of them left.

The shiny object syndrome for me in my story is first I was interested in Profit First because it was going to solve all of my problems. But after we had implemented it, I was on to the next thing, and didn't follow through with actually using Profit First the way it was intended. Sure, the complex business structure was a factor in the failure, but it was my lack of focus that was the real failure. My point is that you may not get it right the first time. Although it can be said that Profit First works 100 percent of the time it is used, you have to *use* it, and use it correctly. You probably will have setbacks and make decisions using your old habits. Keep going!

Now that you have your foundation set and your plan in place, I want to go over some common business situations you will encounter. I've broken this chapter into two parts. The first is Mistakes in Implementation, in other words problems in getting Profit First to work as it is intended. The second section is Roadblocks. Roadblocks are problems you may encounter, even though you are using Profit First correctly.

Mistakes in Implementation

There are three most common mistakes I see when implementing Profit First: getting your bank accounts set up, dipping into the profit account for operating expenses, and not making your transfers/allocations.

1. Trouble Finding a Bank

Finding a bank to facilitate Profit First can be a challenge. I get it, no one wants to change banks. It is a huge hassle. Many creatives continue to work disproportionately with credit unions. Credit unions are *not* business friendly.

You don't want to do business with the big national and regional banks. They will charge you for each account, and those fees add up. Again, I recommend Relayfi (lets.bankwithrelay.com/core group/) which charges no fees. If you don't use Relayfi, I recommend you find a local community bank. They will probably still look at you funny when you tell them what you want to do and will charge fewer fees than the big banks.

2. Raiding the Profit Account

Once you have your bank accounts set up, your next challenge will probably be staying out of the profit account. Generally speaking, every time you take money out of your profit account to fund your operating expenses, you should view that as a failure. But it is only a failure if you don't learn from it. Why did you have to go back to the proverbial well? Was there a change in the scope of work that you were unable to renegotiate? Did you do a poor job of estimating costs? Maybe your change in TAPs for the quarter was too aggressive.

Figure out where you were wrong, understand the root cause of it, and fix it for next time. Sometimes, you can flip that failure around completely. Consider video producer Nick's situation.

Nick said:

"There have been some occasions where we have pulled a little bit from the profit account. We knew it was an investment that we were making. There were some projects where the client would have been a big client for our portfolio, and we knew couldn't get an extra thousand dollars from them.

"But I knew if I spent that money, the exposure that we'd be able to push would be more than the thousand dollars that we would have had. And that's not something that we just loosely do. It takes a lot of thought and actual strategy to think through.

"How are we going to use this content? What's the portfolio piece? How much can we talk about it? We have only done it two or three times. It's worked every time—we've been able to prove the product that we then ended up putting some money into worked out. But the temptation to go to the profit account definitely is real."

3. Not Making Transfers/Allocations

In order to have money in your profit account, you have to transfer money into it. Starting out, one of the hardest things to remember is to do your transfers. Relax. It's okay if you miss one by a couple days or do it on Tuesday instead of Friday, or if you complete the transfer on the 17th instead of the 15th. Maybe you missed the cycle entirely. The important thing is to get back on track. Don't treat it like you've failed and fall completely off the wagon.

What I'm saying is that if things do go awry, don't panic. Simply make the transfer late, and make sure your next transfer stays on schedule. For instance, if you're two days late making a transfer, stay on the same cycle, and make your next transfer as normal. No need to adjust the amounts.

If you miss a transfer entirely, no harm. You had enough in your accounts to accommodate it. Make your next transfer amount include the one you missed. In other words, you can take your TAPs and compute your transfers on the current amount in the account.

If you need, set reminders on your phone or calendar. You might consider hiring someone to do your bookkeeping. Or you can utilize Relayfi.com to automate your transfers. Just get back on track!

If you don't want to switch banks (and I totally understand why you don't want to), most banks will let you set up automatic transfers between accounts. You will have to do it with fixed amounts, which is a challenge when you want to do percentages. You will have to manually change the amounts on the transfers, which is not ideal, but it is better than not making your allocations! Again, Relayfi allows you to automate percentage transfers, which makes like a lot simpler.

I get it, you have other things to do besides remember to do your allocations. But they are essential to the success of Profit First.

Once you overcome the challenges of implementing Profit First, and you have it working as it was intended, you may still hit snags. I will call these roadblocks, and we'll discuss those next.

Roadblocks

Roadblocks are challenges you may encounter even with Profit First working as it is intended. The three most common I encounter with creative industry businesses are not changing the spending habits in your business, hiring an employee, and buying unnecessary items.

1. Not Changing Spending Habits

As I related in my story above, my biggest challenge was changing my spending habits. This is a common problem for people implementing Profit First initially. By using TAPs, you are going to have to adjust your spending. If your quarterly change in TAPs is small, say 1 percent, you might not notice the change, but eventually, you're going to have to stop spending money somewhere.

This is where being a creative is an advantage! How can you achieve the same results with something different, and less expensive? Is the expense truly necessary? The key here is to not give up on an alternative solution. It is way too easy to say, well, we just have to do this. The point of Profit First is to set the amount of profit up front. What is left over is *all* you have to spend. Yes, you can dip into the profit account to make up, but then you have failed to make the profit goal you set.

At the end of the day, you can only reduce expenses so much. You can't reduce your expenses to zero. Eventually, you will find that in order to make your profit grow, you will have to reevaluate how you price things. Your pricing is a much more powerful tool to increase your profit than reducing expenses.

2. Hiring an Employee

Another common roadblock businesses encounter is the decision to hire an employee, but with Profit First, the decision to hire an employee becomes much simpler. You know the profit that you want to make, so the decision to hire an employee comes down to this question: When does hiring that employee allow you to reach your profit target?

As we discussed in Chapter 4 with the Pareto Principle, you hire an employee when you can no longer do your most valuable work, the 20 percent. You want to hire an employee to do some of the 80 percent work. The 80 percent is different for everybody. For some, it may be administrative tasks like drafting proposals, answering emails and phone calls, or invoicing your customers. For others, it will be things that you can do but aren't as valuable as your 20 percent. That may mean you hire an employee to do editing, content creation, or run a camera.

With any employee hire—part-time, full-time, or contractor—you must be able to replace the cost of the employee with additional profit (unless your goal in hiring them is to simply work less). Let's say you can hire a $50,000 a year employee (don't forget to include the costs of taxes and benefits!). If you generate an additional $50,000 in profit, you are at a "break-even." This does give you the benefit of extra time. If that is your primary goal, not to work as much, then good.

An even better outcome is that you have more time, and the $50,000 employee will generate a multiple of their salary in profit. Your basic benchmark should be 2X, or to put it another way, that employee should generate an additional $100,000 in profit. I use 2X, because if you look at the financial data for any service-based business, that is what other companies achieve.

You achieve this 2X profit by freeing your time to do more valuable work or by taking on more work as a company, because that employee would eliminate a pinch point, a place in operations where you can't produce everything available. You can also increase profit by being able to mark up this person's work (i.e., You pay them $25/hour and then can bill that work to your customers at $75/hour). Another option is that you can do a combination of all three of the approaches noted above!

There is always a learning curve in bringing on an employee. They must learn the way you do things, understand your customers, etc. Traditionally, you won't receive the *full* value of a new employee for a year. That doesn't mean you should wait a full year to receive any benefit. If you are conservative, use a special bank account like I mentioned in Chapter 2 to fund the hire with three to six months of their cost (though I wouldn't wait for six months to make a decision on the hire).

You should have a very good idea after three months about whether the employee was a good hire. When evaluating your hiring decision, I would first look to see if they are a good fit with you and any other members of the team. I discuss this in more detail in Chapter 9, but they have to be a cultural fit first. If the relationship doesn't feel right, trust your gut and part ways. Second, is the employee able to do the work to the standard you've set? The point is to get the work off your plate, and onto theirs. Last, evaluate the employee honestly, by asking yourself the question, is this person going to make me money and make my life easier?

An axiom we live by is hire *slow*, fire *fast*. Hiring slowly is about first making sure you really need the employee and second taking the time to find the right person. In most businesses, finding the right person will take six months. Firing fast is about not hanging on to a bad decision. There is a cognitive bias to holding on to things that we have invested time and money into. You simply can't do that with a bad hire. Cut them loose as soon as you know you have a problem.

When you come to the decision of whether to hire an employee or not, use Profit First to help with your decision. Do you have a clear plan of how that employee is going to make you more profitable? Many businesses skip this step, add employees, and end up actually not making any more money, or worse, making less money than before. You don't want to have that business.

3. Your Toys Need to Pay for Themselves

You can implement Profit First correctly and appear to be using it correctly, but there is a challenge many creatives have, the temptation to buy the newest and greatest technology. When evaluating the decision to purchase new equipment or software, ask yourself a simple question: "Will this make me more profit?" If you are not clear on specifically *how* the purchase will increase your profit, don't buy it. There is no hard and fast rule here, but I typically make this decision in my company by looking at the return on investment (ROI). Let's say I'm looking at new software. I will look at how much time it will save and use that to determine how much in wages I will save with the software and compare it to the cost of the software. For instance, say the software costs $20,000 a year, but it saves me from hiring an employee that would cost me $40,000 a year. The return on the investment in the software is 200 percent ($40,000/$20,000). Not every decision will be that clear cut, but this example will help you make those decisions. Not every investment will result in cost savings.

Sometimes the investment is to allow you to produce something more, an increase in revenue. Maybe the investment is in a new type of equipment that allows you to offer a service you don't currently provide. The decision is the same; you simply replace the cost savings with the increased revenue. So, if you wanted to buy equipment for $10,000 that would allow you to earn $20,000 more in revenue, then your return on investment would again be 200 percent. When evaluating revenue increases, first be conservative in your estimate of potential revenue. Second, use the same time frame to compare cost and revenue. If the equipment is realistically going to be outdated in three years, compare that cost to the increased revenue for the next three years.

Without a plan and a set of criteria, you're likely to spend where you need not. After all, we all make purchase decisions emotionally then we justify our emotions with reasons. You need to flip the script on that. There must be a specific reason (increased profit and/or time) to justify a purchase. Leave your wants and desires for your quarterly profit distributions. You will be shocked when the thing you just *had to have* and paid from your operating account becomes not that cool when you have to forgo your family vacation to buy it!

Chris the videographer said it best. Before Profit First, when he was paid for a large job, his first thoughts went to new equipment.

"Honestly, I say we creators almost act like children when it comes to our money. When it comes in, we spend it. We like to invest in new equipment and new fun toys, and we don't really think about the future or have a plan for any kind of down month."

Several creatives we work with actually look at their equipment as a separate business. Kyle, the director of photography, has this experience.

"But then there's this whole other field of owner-operators, which have amassed a certain amount of equipment to get the job done at whatever capacity that they do most often. I was going through an insurance policy early this year and realized that I have amassed roughly $200,000 to 250,000 worth of gear that rents out for X amount on each job. Most of my peers just lump this big number and send the invoice off. My labor rate is $X for the ten hours that gets put on. And then if all my big equipment's going out, you can make another $Y a day just renting out that equipment.

"I wasn't valuing my time always in the equation. *I'll just let my labor rate go for what they want. I'll just make it up with equipment.* But in reality, I wasn't thinking about how much that equipment costs. I wasn't thinking about the replacement cost of it either.

"Now I will discount my gear before I move on to my rate and I most likely won't move on rate anymore because the gear needs to operate completely separately. Now that gear is working to pay business expenses, things like insurance. It's just operating as this extra income source, and I'm thinking of it as a separate business within the business so I'm looking at it from invoice to invoice, like I can purchase another camera body, or I shouldn't be purchasing a lot of gear because I haven't made a lot on the rentals."

That's some next level stuff right there!

Just like with the decision to hire any employee, before you spend large amounts of money on an item, equipment, or software, have a clear plan on how that item is going to increase your profit. If the plan isn't clear, you're likely better off not making the investment.

Summary

When implementing and using Profit First, you may have setbacks. I sure did! The important thing is to learn from your mistakes and go back to the principles of Profit First and make sure you are using it properly.

In this chapter we discussed the common problems you are likely to encounter, and how to overcome them. Those common roadblocks are as follows:

- Implementation Mistakes
  - Trouble finding a bank
  - Raiding the profit account
  - Not making transfers/allocations
- Roadblocks
  - Not changing spending habits
  - Hiring an employee
  - Your toys need to pay for themselves

If you run into something I didn't cover or have a question about implementation, please shoot me an email at profitfirst@coregroupus.com.

In the next chapter, we will discuss things that you will need for a profitable business in addition to Profit First.

Chapter 7:
What Profit First Doesn't Do

To recap what we've covered so far, we talked about why your finances may not be what you want, and how Profit First can fix that. We've discussed the principles behind profit first and all of its components, and how to use Profit First to increase your profit and give you financial clarity. We did a deep dive into your most powerful profit maximizer, your pricing, and how to use your peers' financial information to benchmark your profit potential. In the last chapter, we worked through the places where people have trouble with implementing Profit First, and the most common problems you may encounter and how Profit First helps you solve them.

Now that you know what you can do with Profit First, it's worthwhile to discuss what Profit First does *not* do. Let me begin by asking you a question. What happens if you do things differently? Your morning routine is the same most mornings, and when you are in a hurry and get out of your routine what happens? You forget to brush your teeth. Habits are important for everyone, but for people with creative minds, they are essential. I don't default to being organized, so I rely heavily on routines. My life would be even more chaos without them. The same is doubly true for your business.

Think of processes as routines for your business. You've probably already figured out processes for how you do your operations, although you may not call them processes, and they may not be written down. But regardless of what they're called or how they're communicated, there is a way, a process, for how you do things.

It should be evident that your business needs processes around money. The first process should be Profit First, but it doesn't stop there. In this chapter we'll discuss the three other processes you need to have to ensure a sustainable, profitable business.

Bookkeeping Process

The second process you need in place directly after Profit First is a bookkeeping system. I know, I know that sounds awful, but it is absolutely necessary. Profit First is an awesome process, but it lacks some fundamental things, one of which is bookkeeping. Unfortunately, you can't look at your operating account and tell you how much you spent on software last year.

This is because while Profit First gives you a snapshot of your business at any specific time, it lacks detail, and it is not useful when trying to figure out what has happened in the past. You need this information for two things.

First, and this applies to everyone, you need to have books for tax compliance. Second, you need this information to make business decisions for the future. I'll discuss this in further detail in the Projecting Cash Flow section in Chapter 9.

Again, you must have a bookkeeping process. I don't care if you use green ledger paper, Excel, or QuickBooks. You must have a bookkeeping process in place to capture this information. Fortunately, Profit First perfectly facilitates a good bookkeeping process. The Profit First system sets you up to have a good bookkeeping system in place where you have timely, accurate, and complete financial reporting for your business.

Financial reporting at a minimum looks like monthly income statements. Ideally, financial reporting will include your balance sheet and cash flow statements with all of the supporting detail (e.g., general ledger). You may start with the minimum, but as you work through Profit First and make increasingly difficult and complex business decisions, you will need to move to the ideal. When you make difficult or complex business decisions—like tax planning—spreadsheets and other manual processes will become cumbersome and lack all of the detail you need. You can use software like QuickBooks or Xero, but I recommend that you outsource your bookkeeping to a company like Core.

Timely means that you can have access to last month's information no later than the 10th of the following month. *Accurate* means that it is substantially free from error. This doesn't mean chasing pennies in a bank reconciliation or inventorying paper clips. *Substantially* means that everything meaningful is correct. *Complete* means you are capturing all of the data. Did you record the random business expense paid on your personal credit card? What about the cash expenses?

Many creatives turn to an outside professional for help. Finding competent bookkeeping help is becoming harder and harder. Trust me, we know; we're in the business of employing them. You may be able to find a remote or local bookkeeper that can assist you with this. Alternatively, you can use a company that handles all of the bookkeeping for you. I should note that most companies or firms that do bookkeeping do not do your invoicing. This is usually retained by you, since it likely needs your input.

If you decide to hire someone to do your bookkeeping, the most important trait to look for is communication. You might think it would be attention to detail or something like that, but if you can't understand what the hell they're talking about, you will have a big problem.

I understand that a bookkeeping process is not a sexy business thing, but it is foundational to your financial success. Don't skip putting a process in place.

Tax Compliance Process

The next process you need external support for is taxes. Although you don't need to outsource your bookkeeping, you want your taxes done by a third-party person or company. You aren't going to take the time to learn the income tax code. Again, look for communication skills. Do they listen to you, do they understand your business and your goals? Any trained person can put numbers in a tax software, but only someone that listens to you can give you good advice.

In most states, there is no licensing requirement to prepare income taxes. That's right. You might need a license to cut someone's hair or do their nails, but not to prepare a tax return. Look for either an Enrolled Agent (EA) or a Certified Public Accountant (CPA), and steer away from the H&R Blocks and TurboTaxes of the world. This stuff is just too complicated and ever-changing to trust to just anyone.

Most states don't charge sales tax on services and other creative endeavors, though some states do require you to charge sales tax on certain services. If your state isn't currently, great, but I expect that more and more states will make you in the future. They gotta make that bread!

You likely have outsourced your income tax preparation to someone else, but you should evaluate that relationship and make sure that you have the right partner. Consider discussing some of the tax strategies I discuss in the next chapter with them and see what they recommend for your business. If they haven't already recommended them to you, ask them why not? It may be time for a change.

Payroll Process

Another important process not covered under Profit First relates to payroll, which obviously doesn't apply to everyone. For those who do have employees, you should know that if you have employees or if you do choose to pay yourself as an employee of your company, you must have a payroll process. Payroll taxes and compliance shut down more businesses than income taxes, by far. Businesses forget to file returns, they forget to pay their withholding taxes, or worse, spend the money and don't have the money to pay. There are too many service offerings at a reasonable price to even consider doing payroll yourself. To add to the complexity, many creatives work in a lot of different locations. This can open you up to very complicated payroll situations.

Although Profit First helps you with payroll (e.g., payroll bank account), it doesn't cover all of what you need to do. You have to do things in a timely fashion, pay your taxes, and file your taxes, and they're not always at the same times.

Federal taxes include the payment of federal withholding and FICA taxes. You either have to pay them on the 15th of the following month using the Electronic Filing and Tax Payment System (EFTPS), or—if your total taxes exceed $50,000 for the year—semi-weekly. These taxes are reported on form 941, which is filed quarterly. You also have the Federal Unemployment Tax which is paid quarterly and filed annually on Form 940.

Then you have state (and in some cases local) filing requirements which include state income tax withholding and unemployment taxes. Why do you want to do this yourself again?

You will need a process to ensure that the taxes are paid in a timely manner, and the returns filed on time. Good luck with that.

I will reiterate, if you have employees or are paying yourself as a W-2 employee, outsource your payroll. The risk is not worth the potential costs of your doing your payroll yourself.

Summary

In order to have a financially successful business, you need more than Profit First. Profit First is an awesome tool but has its limitations. In this chapter, we discussed the things that you need *in addition* to Profit First to have complete control over your finances. These processes are:

- Bookkeeping process
- Tax compliance process
- Payroll process, if you have employees or pay yourself as one

In the next chapter, we discuss some powerful income tax strategies you can use right now to put more money in your pocket.

Chapter 8:
Income Tax Strategies for Creatives

Profit First provides a tool to make sure you've set aside money to pay your taxes via the tax bank account, but it doesn't tell you how to pay less tax. In Profit First, there are no "right" tax choices, rather the process makes sure that you have the money to pay them. In the previous chapter, one thing we discussed was that Profit First businesses should seek external help for their taxes. Taxes are probably the least sexy thing, even for accountants. That being said, as you evaluate your profit outcomes pursuant to your business taxes, bear in mind that it is not what you make, but what you *keep* that truly matters.

In the context of tax professionals, they often don't consider the client's business needs when making recommendations. Your tax decisions should not drive business decisions. Too often I've talked to owners that said, "Well, my accountant told me to do that to lower my taxes." One common example is accountant's advice to buy equipment at year end to lower taxes. Stupid. First, you make your business decisions and then find the most efficient tax strategy to implement it. If there is not a clear business reason to do something, then don't do it. Profit First!

To enable your learning on this subject, in this chapter I outline some of my favorite tax strategies that are great alternatives for creatives to consider. Although I outline some great tax strategies here, I do not recommend you try them yourself. Tax laws change, your situation is unique, and I'm not putting all of the caveats in here. This is merely a starting point for you to have the discussion with your tax professional (remember what we discussed about Tax Process in the previous chapter).

But first, before I go into tax strategies, I want to cover a topic that many creatives have questions about, LLCs.

LLCs

Creative businesses often come to us with the question, should I have an LLC? I do recommend that you form a separate legal entity such as an LLC for your business. I'm not a lawyer, and I'm not giving legal advice; I'm speaking from experience as a fellow creative. There are compelling reasons to keep your business and personal finances separate, both tax and legal.

When you form an LLC for your business, you will have to retitle your bank accounts, and in some cases, you'll have to actually change your bank accounts to the LLC. It is a great idea to do this all at once when you are setting up Profit First if you haven't already formed an LLC.

So, let's discuss the tax implications of forming an LLC for your creative business. When you form an LLC with your state's Secretary of State, for instance, that in and of itself does nothing for your taxes. In fact, the IRS has no idea you created it. In order to take any tax advantages of having a separate legal entity, you will need to do some additional things.

The IRS will default to treating you as a sole proprietor if you have only one member. This means that you will file your business taxes on your personal tax return (i.e., form 1040) with a schedule C. The tax problem with that is that your entire profit from your business will be subject to self-employment tax at a current rate of 15.3 percent.

An alternative tax election can have you file that LLC business return separate from your personal return as an S-Corporation. I'll discuss below the benefits of choosing this tax strategy, but those are your two options for an LLC, be taxed as a sole proprietor or an S-Corporation.

So, which is best for you? Here are some tax strategies for you to consider in your decision. Generally, I don't recommend that you consider electing to be taxed as an S-Corporation until your profit is above $40,000, but understand that tax laws change, so consult a tax professional.

I've divided the tax strategies into three categories, those applicable to Sole Proprietors, those applicable to S-Corporations, and those applic-able to both.

The tax strategies we will cover are:

- For Sole Proprietors
    - Using Section 105 plans to deduct medical expenses
    - Hiring your child to generate tax deductions and no income to them
- For S-Corporations
    - Lowering your self-employment tax
    - Renting your home to generate tax-free income
- Applicable to both
    - Paying for college and making it a business deduction
    - Combining business and personal travel

Using individual 401ks to lower taxes

Sole Proprietor

Remember from the above discussion about LLCs that even though you form an LLC, the IRS will default to taxing you as a Sole Proprietor if you don't make an election. A sole proprietor is reported and taxed on your personal return on Schedule C of Form 1040. If your return has a Schedule C for your creative business, then these strategies apply to you.

1. Section 105 Plan

A Section 105 Plan is an employer-sponsored health plan that allows sole proprietors to deduct 100 percent of their medical expenses, including health insurance premiums, as a business expense. The plan is named after Section 105 of the Internal Revenue Code, which governs the tax treatment of employer-provided health plans.

In essence, a Section 105 Plan allows a sole proprietor to write off the cost of their medical insurance premiums and other deductible medical expenses as business expenses, reducing their taxable income and saving money on taxes.

The plan must be set up properly to comply with IRS rules and regulations, which include:

- The plan must be in writing and establish eligibility requirements for participation.
- The plan must provide benefits to all eligible employees (if any).
- The plan must not discriminate in favor of highly compensated employees (not applicable if you don't have any employees).
- The plan must be funded solely by the employer.
- The plan must provide benefits that are exclusively for the purpose of reimbursing medical expenses.

The 105 plan allows sole proprietors to customize their health benefits to suit their needs, rather than being limited to the plans offered by insurance carriers Another benefit of a Section 105 Plan is that it can be used to cover a wide range of medical expenses, including deductibles, copays, prescriptions, and even some alternative therapies not covered by insurance. This can be especially valuable for individuals with chronic health conditions or who require expensive medical treatments.

Download sample section 105 plan document at www.profitfirst4creatives.com/resources

---

2. Hiring Your Child

If you have children under the age of eighteen you can hire them and their wages will be exempt from Social Security tax, Medicare tax, and FUTA tax. The FUTA tax exemption lasts until the employee-child reaches age twenty-one. They can be part-time, full-time, or whatever works for you and the child, but they must be paid less than $1,000/mo.

The standard deduction in 2022 for a single person was $12,950; there-fore, your child will owe nothing to the feds on the first $12,950 of wages, unless the kid has income from other sources. Bonus tip, your kid can then set aside some or all of the wages and contribute money to a Roth IRA or 529 college fund. Although I don't cover tax strate-gies about IRAs and 529 plans in this book, they are additional tax savings opportunities.

Even if the child crosses the standard deduction threshold on their earned income for the year, their tax bracket is likely lower than yours so it will still be lowering the family tax load. You get a business tax deduction (employee wages) for money you might have shoveled out to the child anyway. It reduces your federal income tax, self-employment tax, and state income tax (if any).

An example of this strategy might look like hiring your teenage child to help with web design or social media. Use your imagination. You will save taxes while teaching your child valuable skills, including how to be an entrepreneur!

One last note on this strategy. You may be asking if there are legal issues with employing minors. According to the Federal Department of Labor, children are exempt from labor laws if they are working in a business solely owned by their parents. Of course, you may have ethical qualms with requiring your children to work in your business, but I'll leave that to you to work out for yourself.

Now let's look at the strategies for those of you who have (or are considering) an S-Corporation. And don't forget to review the strategies that are applicable to both Sole Proprietors and S-Corporations that follow.

S-Corporation

As I mentioned above, if the profit from creative business is near $40,000 a year, it is time to consider an S-Corporation. Using an S-Corporation is one of the most powerful strategies to lower your income subject to self-employment taxes, and thus your overall tax bill.

1. Lowering Self-Employment Tax

Let's start by defining what self-employment (SE) tax is. According to the IRS website SE tax is a tax consisting of Social Security and

Medicare taxes primarily for individuals who work for themselves. Generally, if you have net earnings in excess of $400, you have to pay self-employment taxes.

The SE tax rate is 15.3 percent, which mirrors the tax an employee and employer would pay for FICA if you worked for someone else. But you do receive one-half of that expense against your income tax, which is equivalent to the employer's portion. This is a deduction against your taxable income for regular taxes, *not* the SE tax.

As a sole proprietor, all of the profit from your business is subject to SE tax. In many cases, the amount of self-employment tax is more than the amount of the income tax! Using an S-Corporation, which doesn't pay self-employment tax on its profit, you can lower your overall taxes.

The creative working in the S-Corporation has to take a salary from the corporation, like a regular employee. This will cause the owner to pay FICA taxes on those wages, which is the same rate as the SE tax (15.3 percent). However, any profit *above* the salary amount is no longer subject to the SE tax. Understand, it is still subject to income tax, but you've saved 15.3 percent from being a sole proprietor (Schedule C)!

So, let's say you have a small business that generates $70k in net income after expenses. As a schedule C sole proprietor, you will pay 15.3 percent SE tax or $10,700. This is in addition to income taxes (which I've excluded from this example). So now, let's say you incorporate that business and elect S-Corporation status. You take a salary of $35k and pay the FICA tax on that wage equal to $5,350 and have net income of $35k after the salary. That net income is not subject to SE tax, saving you $5,350! Voilà!

The more astute of you may be asking, so why not just take no salary and save even more? Good question. Because the IRS expressly prohibits it, that's why. The IRS says that everyone working in the business must be paid a reasonable salary. So, what is a reasonable salary?

There are a lot of factors that the IRS could consider, but the overall premise comes down to, are you paying yourself market wages? In other words, if you were to pay someone to do what you are doing for the business, what would you have to pay them? Business owners who wear multiple hats have a hard time clearly defining that. Is the wage one I would pay a graphic designer, an SEO specialist, a salesperson, a bookkeeper? You get the picture.

My general advice is don't get greedy and do consult a tax professional to work through your individual situation. Whatever you do, don't take zero. There is a separate line item on S-Corporation tax returns for officer's compensation. Leaving this line blank or zero is an increased risk of audit.

2. Rent Your Home

When I tell creatives about this tax strategy, they usually don't believe it. I admit it is a kind of crazy loophole. It is named the Augusta Rule (after Augusta Golf Club members who had a good congressional lobbyist) or Code Section 280a, if you're going to go looking for the citation.

The rule says that anyone renting their personal residence out for fewer than fifteen days a year doesn't have to include the income for taxes. Now, you don't get to take any deductions against that income, but who cares? It's tax-free money.

So how do you use it for your business? The S-Corporation rents your residence from you for no more than fourteen days. The S-Corporation receives a tax deduction while you receive the income tax free. Although there is no limit to the amount of income you can exclude, the rent has to be based upon the market. Unless you live in Laguna Nigel, you can't charge the company $5k a day.

You will need to have good documentation as to the rental agreement, as well as the business purpose of the rental. You can't use your residence for entertainment purposes and use this exemption, except for employees (e.g., Christmas party). But you can use it for business meetings. Just make sure you've documented it!

Renting your home to your S-Corporation is an uber-easy way to generate non-taxable income. Don't ignore it.

Applicable to Both Sole Proprietors and S-Corporations

There are some tax strategies that apply to both Sole Proprietors and S-Corporations. Here are my favorites:

1. Paying for College

This strategy is a twist on the Hiring Your Child above. Although it does apply to both sole proprietors and S-Corporations, there are additional advantages when applied to sole proprietors.

With this strategy, the business pays your child, regardless of age, to do work for the business. It needs to be project work, and not ongoing. Because the work is not continuous, it is not subject to self-employment tax. So, the one-time task could be to work on your website, create videos, paint your office. Things like that. You just don't want them to have continuous work or treat them as an employee.

Your child will receive a 1099-MISC from your business and report this income on their tax return. They, depending on the amount, pay no taxes (if they are below the standard deduction amount) or less income tax than you would because they are in a lower tax bracket. As a bonus to this strategy, you can use this income to allow them to make either a regular IRA contribution or contribute to a Roth IRA. Of course, with the Roth IRA, there is no tax deduction, but if they are going to make a regular IRA contribution, you can compensate them more without their having to pay taxes.

Although this strategy is ostensibly for paying for college, it can also be used to shift income to your child to take advantage of their lower tax bracket as well.

2. Combining Business and Personal Travel

The general rule is that you can deduct travel for business if ordinary and necessary, and the courts have defined these terms very broadly. The key components the IRS will consider when determining if the travel qualifies as a business deduction are as follows:

- Profit Motive: Essentially you need to show how the travel will make you money. The profit doesn't have to be immediate, and really doesn't even have to materialize. But you have to have justification that the travel more likely than not would result in extra profit.
- Stay Overnight: You have to stay overnight.
- "For Only" Test: Would a rational businessperson make this only trip for business reasons?
- Primary Purpose Test: Easy way to do this is to make the majority of your trip business days. Travel days can be counted as business days in most cases.
- Maintain Good Records: Duh! This includes keeping records for each separate expenditure while away from home, the date of departure and return, the number of days spent on business, where you went, and the business reason for travel.

What happens if you have personal days before, after, or in between business days? While you can't write off the expenses for the personal days (e.g., hotel), you still can deduct your transportation costs in total. We find that most creatives can find ways to justify days as business days, however, and eliminate this problem.

Combine your business and personal travel to take all of the legitimate tax deductions you can.

3. Individual 401k

Setting up an individual 401k has many retirement and tax advantages. I recommend that every creative create wealth outside of their business. When it comes to retirement accounts, 401ks are hands down the best option. Don't have any employees but yourself? No problem! That's where the individual 401k comes in.

If you have no employees, you can create an individual 401k account with most brokerage companies. Understand, you *can't* have any employees except your spouse. If you have employees, you will have to have a "full" 401k which has additional testing and filing requirements as well as additional costs.

401k accounts have higher limits than other retirement plans like SIMPLE IRAs or SEPs, allowing you to take a larger tax deduction. Additionally, with 401ks, you can have a Roth provision. This is great if you want to contribute to a Roth IRA, but otherwise can't because of the income limitations. The 401k Roth has no income limitations. Bonus! You can contribute to *both* your 401k Roth and an individual Roth. Double sweet!

Last, 401ks allow for loans. This means that you can borrow money from yourself. You do have to pay the money back, with interest, within five years via payroll deductions. But the loan allows you to take money out of your retirement account without having to pay taxes on it.

Setting up an individual 401k is not just a great way to minimize your taxes, it also provides you a way to build wealth outside of your business to provide for retirement.

Open an individual 401k account without costs and start making contributions to it.

4. Home Office Deduction

This tax strategy is available to both Sole Proprietorships and S-Corporations but is ideal for those of you who don't have a separate office and are primarily working from home. Over the years, the home office deduction has received a bad rap, and many people avoid it. You shouldn't! It is a legitimate business deduction that can save you money on your taxes. In a nutshell, if you have a qualifying home office, you can deduct the expenses associated with it. There are some possible complications when you go to sell your home (if you own it) that we will not cover here, so discuss the options with your tax professional before you take the deduction.

A qualified home office is one that:

- Is used exclusively and regularly for business.
- Is your principal place of business.

If you have a qualifying space, then you can deduct a pro rata share of all expenses:

- Insurance
- Repairs and maintenance
- Utilities
- Home association dues
- Security
- Real estate taxes (if you own your home)
- Depreciation (if you own your home)
- Mortgage interest (if you own your home)
- Rent

Pro rata simply means the percentage of your home office space compared to the whole house. If your office is 200 square feet, and your home is 2,000 square feet, you can deduct 10 percent of the applicable expenses. There is a simplified method the IRS allows that is a flat dollar amount that you multiply by the home office square footage to determine the deduction. If you own your home, I don't recommend the simplified method, because it doesn't include depreciation or interest, which is usually a substantial amount.

Make sure your tax accountant is helping you with your home office deduction. It is a powerful way to lower your income tax bill.

We covered a lot of ground, and you have a lot to discuss with your tax accountant. It doesn't matter what the time of the year is, get started by scheduling a call today.

Summary

Although Profit First doesn't specifically address lowering your tax bill with proper planning, it does give you the very important tool of setting aside money to pay your taxes via the tax account. Creative business owners need to first decide if they want a separate legal entity for their business, like an LLC. Then they need to weigh the pros and cons of the tax implications of whether they want to be taxed as a Sole Proprietor or an S-Corporation.

We've outlined some tax strategies to consider depending on where your business is. To recap:

- Using S-Corporations to lower your self-employment tax
- Utilizing Section 105 Plans
- Hiring your child
- Renting your home
- Paying for your kid's college
- Combining business and personal travel
- Opening individual 401ks
- Using home office deduction

Use them as a starting point for conversations with your tax professional. Please do not attempt to implement them yourself.

In the next chapter, we go HAM and take it to the next level with advanced concepts.

Chapter 9: Advanced Concepts (HAM Chapter)

HAM, for those of you out of the know, is what my kids (ages twenty-nine, twenty-seven, and twenty-three at the time of this book) say when they "go hard" as in they go "Hard as a Mother f#$%@r" or HAM. I swear, if I didn't have children, I would be lost.

Profit First is a simple tool and works 100 percent of the time it is used (properly). This chapter is beyond Profit First. It assumes that you have properly implemented Profit First and have used it to obtain the profit that you want. Working with a tax professional, you've maximized your tax savings. Now what?

I'm including this chapter to share experiences from my business journey that I hope will help you take your business beyond what you've accomplished. If you've achieved the above, you have put yourself in rarefied air, among the top 10 percent of business owners, so if you want to skip this chapter, I'm fine with that.

In this chapter, we're going to cover:

- Business with a partner
- Projecting cash flow
- Stages of growth using the entrepreneurial operating system (EOS)
- Building a business to sell

Businesses with Partners

My attorney likes to say having business partners is like being married, except you don't get to have sex. Ouch! Most of the time, I see people starting a business as partners because there is a perceived synergy in skills and interests. One person is the uber-creative, while the other has more business acumen. I believe partnerships *can* work, but they come with complications. Sometimes those complications aren't worth it.

Be very clear on why you are considering a partner and have a clear understanding of each of your roles and responsibilities. It wouldn't be a bad idea to actually create a job description for each of you. Plan for the ending—it will happen. The best time to do this is at the outset of the venture. Document this in an operating agreement for LLC or a shareholder agreement for corporations. Make sure this document covers the following contingencies:

- **Death or Incapacity of a Partner:** Although the legal entity will continue with the death or incapacity of a partner, you want to agree on what happens in those events. For instance, if you are in a coma, can your partner make business decisions without you? If your partner dies, you will be dealing with their successor (spouse, children). Do you want to be in business with them? Probably not.
  I recommend determining a purchase price (or a method of determining the business price) and putting it in the agreement. I also recommend funding this purchase with life and/or disability insurance. This provides the funds to buy the partner out in the event of death or disability and makes the transition smoother. The proceeds of the insurance and subsequent payout to the surviving spouse would flow through the operating account.
- **Buy/Sell:** What if one of you wants out? You probably don't want your partner to sell to somebody else. The buy/sell provisions spell out what happens when someone wants to get out of the business. Again, I recommend either establishing a purchase price or a methodology of determining the price in the agreement. One way to do this is the so-called

"push-pull" provision. This basically says that a partner can offer to sell their interest in the company for a price, but if the other partner(s) doesn't want to buy, the original partner has to agree to buy their interest for the same amount. This keeps everyone honest on the valuation.

- **Third-Party Offer:** What happens if a third party offers to buy the company, but your partner doesn't want to? There is a legal provision called drag-along that allows majority owners to force the minority owners to sell. Alternatively, you can work out some other terms in the agreement to address this potential.

- **Operational Control:** Often times, I see fifty-fifty partnerships. This is not a good idea. If the owners can't agree, the business maintains the status quo. This is a recipe for stagnation, especially if you and your partner are not in lockstep as to how the business should proceed. In my case, my brother was a minority owner, and I could override him, but often times, I didn't want to proceed without his commitment. Don't put yourself in this situation. The agreement can state that one partner has operational or managerial control of this business. Egos can come into play here, and it may be difficult for one of you to take a back seat. If nothing else, have one owner have 51 percent ownership. This sets the expectation up front that there aren't going to be any ties.

These are all essential aspects to address or at least consider regardless of whether they're a major feature of your business or are not attended to at all. It is better to have these conversations up front than a few years down the line. Going through this exercise, you may find that you don't really want a partner!

Having a business partner is not necessary to have a financially successful business. If you decide to have, or already have, a partner in your business, it is imperative to put down the essentials above in the proper documentation. Don't wait until there is a problem; schedule a call with your business attorney today. What if you already have a partner and they aren't on board with Profit First? I think it is important for you to be equally yoked when it comes to finances. If your partner is spending money like a drunken sailor and you're trying to implement Profit First, it isn't going to work.

If your partner isn't the numbers person, and they say do whatever you want, it might work. Alternatively, if they are the numbers person, you definitely need to get them on board before proceeding with implementing Profit First. Profit First is a fundamental change in the business. It's on par with saying I think we should change our target customer. You really need to be in agreement for you to be successful. Hopefully, you both want to make more profit, but you may have some selling to do. You may have to review Chapter 1 with them and have some difficult conversations. In the end, I would recommend going in different directions and separate if you can't agree. Eventually, you're going to have a big conflict on the subject. Best to preserve what you have and move on.

Forecasting Cash Flow

Probably the biggest challenge with growing a business is predicting cash flow. This may sound like too big of a challenge, but I promise I'll show you an easy way to do it. One of the things I absolutely *love* to do (no, seriously, I love it) is to take a business's operational plan and turn it into numbers. To me numbers are a type of language, the language of business. Taking the business plan and translating to numbers provides valuable insights—you can see things that you don't see in words.

For instance, let's say that you want to merge or purchase another creative business. You have a written plan of what that looks like. You think that you can sell your services to their customers and eliminate certain employees because of redundancies. Putting that plan into a forecast, let's see what the numbers look like if everything goes according to plan. Additionally, if things don't go as planned, you will know quickly, comparing your forecast with actual financial performance.

Many of you may have tried budgets for your business. Budgets simply don't work for small businesses. Budgets were made for larger businesses as a means of accountability and control. When you're the owner, and you're not going to control yourself or hold yourself accountable, then what is the point of a budget?

Instead, I recommend creating a forecast. I keep a rolling twelve-month forecast for my business. A rolling twelve simply means you always have a twelve-month forecast. When one month ends, you add a month to the end. This is better than setting a twelve-month plan at the beginning of the year, and the wheels fall off. You planned on landing a big customer in the first quarter and it didn't happen. Your forecast for the rest of the year is now junk. A rolling twelve-month ensures you always have something usable and up to date.

When I create a forecast, I start with the revenue projections for the next twelve months. What is the planned growth? Ideally this will be tied into a specific marketing plan, not just I think we'll grow 10 percent this year.

Once you have the revenue nailed down, I move to variable costs. Since we will be using Real Revenue, we don't need to worry about flow-through costs to contractors, because that's excluded. So, what are your other variable costs? If I bring another $1,000 in real revenue, what costs will change? Will you have to buy additional software licenses or hire an extra crew? Here I don't count any additional money spent on advertising or marketing. Just your operational costs.

Then you have your fixed costs, like insurance or rent. Generally, you don't need to do anything with these, but *all* costs are variable over time. At some point, you will need additional space, added phone lines, etc. But for this exercise, we're going to assume that a lot of your costs aren't going to change, unless you're planning on reducing them with your TAPs.

Before we put it all together, consider whether you will need to hire an employee. Again, at some point in this exercise, you will have to because of your time constraints. Will you be able to handle the growth for the next twelve months by yourself?

Last, we want to figure out our marketing costs. When I ask virtually any business owner what their cost is to acquire a new customer, they look at me with a blank face. I assume that's because most business owners don't have a very clear marketing plan and strategy, nor do they have good financial processes to track those costs. Sometimes, they have this information, but they have never actually calculated their acquisition costs.

To plan for growth, it is critical to know the cost of acquisition, and put it into your forecast plan. For virtually all creatives, their marketing acquisition costs are small compared to the added profit new customers create. This is probably why they've never considered it. It is still important to consider if you want to have scalable growth. You want a marketing machine where you can put $1 in and get $2 out.

So now that you have all of these items, this is what it will look like. In this fictional business plan, we're projecting revenue to increase $5,000 per month, and our variable costs to increase by only $1,000 per month because we're going to have to hire a part-time employee to help with the work. Our fixed costs are going to remain the same, and we're going to spend $500/month to attract this new revenue. We are going to start in January, so we will spend the marketing dollars, but won't see any new revenue from that until the next month. This forecast shows that our profit is going to go up by $4,500 per month in three months. I'm including all of the owner's compensation TAP and tax TAP in the fixed account line.

REVENUE FORECAST

	JANUARY	FEBRUARY	MARCH	3 MONTH TOTAL
• REAL REVENUE	10,000	15,000	15,000	40,000
• LESS: VARIABLE EXPENSES	(1,000)	(2,000)	(2,000)	(5,000)
• LESS: FIXED COSTS	(5,000)	(5,000)	(5,000)	(15,000)
• LESS: MARKETING COSTS	(500)	(500)	(500)	(1,500)
• PROFIT	3,500	7,500	7,500	18,500

The astute observer will say that our profit only went up $4,000 per month ($7,500 less $3,500), but we have to add back in the new marketing spend that we didn't have at the beginning. In other words, $500 per month, or $1,500 for three months, produced an increase in revenue of $4,500 or a 300 percent return on our marketing investment. Not too shabby.

This forecast does two things. First, it is a way to see where potential problems in your plan are with your profit and cash flow. Second, it gives you an additional sanity check when looking at your bank accounts. Using this forecast, I would expect $18,500 to be in my profit account at the end of the quarter.

Commit to creating a forecast for your business, even if it's for the next ninety days. You will be amazed at what it does for your business.

Trailing Twelve-Month Income Statement

Now that you have your forecast, it is time to compare it to actual results to see if the plan actually worked. We do this using a rolling twelve-month, or in this case three-month, income statement. Simply, this is the last twelve months (or three months) of operations. For example, for April of this year, we're looking at results from May of last year through April of this year. By comparing income statements this way, we see a more accurate picture of the financial performance of the business. It eliminates any seasonality, and smooths out any timing differences, such as annual payments.

Let's continue the above example and see how the business did. Notice below, that these numbers are for three months, not the one month in the above table. I'm doing this because I want to see the trends, or the changes by month. To see if our plan worked as expected, I'm going to compare the three months that ended with March with our three-month total column above.

3 MONTH INCOME STATEMENT

	3 MONTHS END JANUARY	3 MONTHS END FEBRUARY	3 MONTHS END MARCH
• REVENUE	30,000	32,000	39,000
• EXPENSES			
• VARIABLE EXPENSES	(4,000)	(5,000)	(6,000)
• FIXED COSTS	(15,000)	(15,000)	(15,000)
• MARKETING COSTS	(500)	(1,000)	(1,500)
• (PROFIT)	10,500	11,500	16,500

Putting the numbers in this format allows you to see changes quickly. First let's look at the forecast for three months and the actual three months ended March, the last column of each table. Revenue was $1,000 less than we projected (40,000 less 39,000) and variable expenses were $1,000 more than we expected (6,000 less 5,000). Our fixed costs were right on target, as were our marketing costs. The shortfall in revenue of $1,000 and the increased variable expense of $1,000 resulted in our profit being $2,000 less than we projected (18,500 less 16,500).

Now we can dig into why we were off from our forecast. In this hypothetical scenario, it turns out that we had found an employee the first month, but we had to hire him right away, instead of waiting until February. Additionally, our marketing efforts weren't as productive as we had hoped, and the new clients came later than we had planned.

In this scenario, we missed our initial forecast, but the trend is good (revenue up, costs up but not out of line) and we made more profit. I would say we successfully implemented our plan, but now we have some additional information to consider when we forecast the next three months.

Combine using your forecast and your rolling income statement to track how you are doing in implementing your business plans. This accountability will keep you from spinning your wheels by making plans and not knowing whether what you are doing is making a difference. Speaking of spinning your wheels, let's talk about the ultimate tool in gaining traction, the Entrepreneurial Operating System (or EOS) and the stages of growth of a business.

Stages of Growth Using the Entrepreneurial Operating System (EOS)

As I told you at the outset, my first goal when I started Core was to just grow. Growth for growth's sake. What else was there? Spoiler alert, that doesn't work. In order to continue to grow your business, you have to have two things: passion and mindset. They are both needed, the absence of either will result in a stall.

Let's start with passion. Remember what Todd Henry said, "Passion is sacrifice." We've already discussed this, but growth is *hard*. If you don't have a burning passion, you will not have the fortitude to deal with these difficulties. If you *do* have the passion, you will figure out a way. It really is that simple. I reached a point where I told my brother, who was my partner at the time, that I don't know what I'm going to do but it isn't going to be running an accounting company.

My passion was gone, or so I thought. I went into the wilderness and attempted a software company startup for two years. After I had "failed" at that, I was sucked back into the business, because it was on a downhill slide. I thought at the time that I would right the ship, and then move on, but something interesting happened along the way.

When I came back to Core, I told my partners that we had to do things differently. It was then that we implemented the Entrepreneurial Operating System (EOS). EOS is a program developed by Gino Wickman and outlined in his book *Traction*. Think of it as an operating system for your business, just like your computer runs on an operating system software.

That was almost eight years ago. My partners left shortly after implementing EOS. As I discussed in Chapter 6, the business just couldn't support three partners and make the money we should by implementing Profit First. My leadership team is all new. Our target market and service offerings are new. In fact, there is very little that has not changed. So, what caused that?

Simply, a change in mindset on my part. There is an article I reference at least once a year by Daniel Marcos (www.profitfirst4creatives.com/resources). He is a co-founder with Verne Harnish (The Growth Guy) of the Growth Institute. In this article, titled "You'll Need to Evolve Yourself if You Want to Scale Your Business," he succinctly outlines the different stages of growth of a business, and what you, as the business owner, have to be in each stage.

I'm going to add to his list by adding an initial stage, but here are the four (five with mine added) stages of business growth:

- Solopreneur: No Employees (my addition)
- Startup: 1-5 Employees
- Grow Up: 6-15 Employees
- Scale Up: 16-250 Employees
- Dominate Your Industry: 250+ Employees

In the article, Marcos then discusses how the business owner will have to grow personally to be able to grow the business to these levels. What worked as a solopreneur will not work as a startup. In many ways, the growth is foundational; in other words, you have to learn the mindset lessons of the prior step to proceed to learn the next.

We at Core are on the Scale Up stage and have been for over ten years. I told you; growth is hard. It wasn't until I understood that I had to change my mindset and grow personally before the company could grow that we finally started getting traction. For us, that began with the implementation of EOS, but really it wasn't EOS per se. It was my admission that something had to change. Something had to be different because what I had been doing wasn't working anymore. Letting go of hard-won things is extremely difficult. In fact, when we implemented EOS, we actually shrunk our company by 20 percent.

We had to prune the tree to allow it to grow healthy. That, on an emotional level, was one of the hardest things I ever had to do. It sucked, big time. Felt like defeat.

I'm going to only discuss the first three stages. I'm doing this because Core is still at the Scale Up stage, and I don't feel like I have mastered it enough to discuss it.

1. Solopreneur (No Employees)

When you start your journey as a creative, you don't have any employees—you're the captain and the crew, a solopreneur. Eventually, you will have to make a decision on whether you want to be limited by yourself, and what you can do yourself. The vast majority of business owners remain at this stage. Remember, this isn't about making it up the ladder to domination. This is about having a realistic map of the journey. I started out with this map, and I got lost and wasted a lot of time and energy. If you are content with your business at this level, congratulations!

2. Startup (1-5 Employees)

Once you have some time under your belt, you're ready to move to Startup. Don't be confused with the term *start-up*, which means a fledgling business. Marcos defines this as any business with fewer than six employees. The term has nothing to do with the length of time you have had your business.

Moving to startup involves others, and frankly this is a difficult choice for most creatives. You can't control everything (like you really controlled any of it at all) if you are working with others. This fear of lack of control holds many back. Of course, some people hire others anyway without changing their mindset. They're usually miserable and make their employees (and everyone else) miserable as well. For me, the hardest part was delegating the work and still being responsible for the results. If something wasn't "right," I wanted to default back to taking back control and doing it myself. I didn't want to be responsible for someone else's mistakes.

The reality was I made mistakes too. I might have been better than my employees at some things, but I couldn't *do* everything myself. This attitude led to my actually telling myself that "I could do everything in the business better than any of my employees." You see what's wrong with that attitude. Although it may have been true in certain circumstances, it wasn't universally true. What hubris! In any case, with that attitude, I could never effectively delegate anything. I made my employees nuts and I was frustrated managing them. That eventually led me to where I left the company for two years.

Using EOS, I was able to effectively delegate work through standardized processes and standardized service offerings. I had the tools to effectively manage and hold the team accountable. We share a common set of values and purpose, so although we do things differently, we're all rowing in the same direction.

Eventually, this allowed me to let loose. Now, I still sometimes see things that I would have done differently, but it doesn't matter. If I want to be at this level of business, I have to be okay with people doing things differently than I do. There is no alternative. Frankly, if you can't give up control, you're going to be more content, and more profitable if you get rid of your employees and work by yourself. Hopefully, you'll make that decision before you start the journey.

If you want to move to the Grow Up stage of growth, you have to hire the right team, and you have to become a leader, not just a manager. Hiring the right team is not just about filling spots to get work done. It is about being very intentional about who you hire. You have to ensure that they are first a cultural fit. They share the same values. Second, they have to be bought into the vision.

3. Grow Up (6-15 Employees)

The decision to move to the Grow Up stage is a challenging one for all entrepreneurs, but especially so for creatives. This move feels to many creatives like it is where things start to feel corporate because the organization grows beyond the direct control of the creative. Decisions are made without the direct input of the owner. In order for you, the creative, to be comfortable with that, you have to focus on building the team.

To move to Grow Up, there is no room on the bus for misfits. As famed author Jim Collins (*Good to Great*) puts it, you must have the right people in the right seats of the bus. The bus is heading somewhere (the vision), and if they don't want to go where you're going, let them off. Once they're on the bus, you have to make sure they're in the right seat/job. Every person that is not on the right bus or in the right seat is a distraction to the driver (you) and will limit your ability to arrive at your destination.

In addition to hiring the right team, you have to become a leader. Management of people is around holding them accountable and keeping them on track, which still needs to be done. But a leader helps their people be successful. Being a leader is about making your team better and inspiring them to the vision. For me, this looks a lot more like coaching than it does anything else. When I have discussions with my direct reports, there is always a management component: making sure that the important things are getting done and that they have the tools they need to succeed.

Many creatives struggle with management and leadership, because we haven't been trained in it. We also tend to have high emotional intelligence, which makes us sensitive to others. This doesn't have to be a barrier—in fact, it is a benefit. Being constructively critical and pushing people to do better was difficult for me at first, because I would put myself in the employee's situation, and feel the criticism myself. Because of this, I would often avoid having those difficult conversations. When I reframed my mindset and understood that those conversations were actually helpful to the employee, I was able to perceive those conversations as positive.

Sometimes the conversations are more in depth. We might discuss whether they are satisfied in their job, personally and professionally. As inspirational leaders, often times people will fill a role because it needs to be done, and because you asked. If they don't *want* the job, the responsibilities, they will eventually fail. I put my brother in that situation, and it damned near ruined our relationship and the company. In the end, he had the courage to decide to leave the job, because God knows I didn't have the guts to fire him.

This type of leadership is scary because it is entirely unpredictable. What happens when that employee says the job no longer fits with what they want? Let's just say that they're going to have that conversation with or without you. It is much better to have the conversation with them and facilitate that exit than it is to have it sprung on you.

Or sometimes, the business has moved on from a tenured employee. What the job requires now has changed from what it was. Are you willing as a leader to have tough conversations with a person who is now a friend? I had to fire an employee who had been with me seventeen years. I had to tell him that we could no longer use him. That sucked. But I was willing to look at the needs of the team ahead of my own discomfort, and his employment. Leaders see the welfare of the whole team above everything else.

This personal growth is difficult. Our brains are hardwired for comfort. If it perceives disruption, it will defend itself, sometimes subconsciously. You may even experience physical symptoms. A great book I recommend on the subject is *The Big Leap* (Hendricks). I've worked with a business coach for the last two years. We meet weekly, and I can tell you that I still struggle with some of the changes. It has led me into some deep personal reflection and work. It has caused me to evaluate other personal relationships, and how I show up there. This is not for the faint of heart.

Had I known the challenges at the outset, would I have still decided to grow? I don't know. I can tell you that the last seven years of the business were harder than the first nineteen. It was harder to grow myself and make the difficult decisions than it was to start the business. Consider that before you begin your journey.

To summarize, you will eventually reach a point where your business cannot go any further. Don't look to external factors when you do. Evaluate yourself and tackle the personal growth necessary. Your business will then grow organically after you have.

Building Your Business to Sell

You probably aren't thinking about the end game, the exit. Certainly, you are not when you're just starting out. At some point, you most likely will. The sooner you start thinking about how to exit the business, the better. Why? Because the changes that you will need to make your business more attractive to sell to another are the exact same things that you need to make your business more profitable and less time-consuming. If you are going to grow your business, why not do it so that it is more valuable *now* and in the future?

For most of you, being solopreneurs, it's no big deal. You probably will be able to find someone like yourself that will cherry-pick your clients and pay you something for it. Just don't rely on that for your retirement. You will need to build wealth outside of your business to provide for that.

When selling a business, there are essentially two types of buyers: cash flow and strategic. Cash flow buyers are looking at the business to repay the investment and make future earnings. Strategic buyers are looking for something that your business has that they need. For instance, maybe they want the expertise of your team, or your book of business, because it compliments their own. Maybe they're buying a bunch of similar businesses with the intention of putting them together, streamlining overhead, and selling to a larger investor.

Your cash flow buyers are going to have a very fixed amount that they are able to pay. The vast majority of business sales have some type of financing. The cash flow from your business must be able to repay the debt in five to seven years, and that is going to be the maximum you can sell it for. A strategic buyer can pay significantly more. Strategic buyers are hard to find, and usually take time to cultivate.

If you have a business with employees, you likely can sell the business intact. Unless you have a business with $1 million in profit, you will be limited in the pool of buyers. Above $1 million in annual profit, you might have other potential strategic buyers. Regardless of your potential buyers, you have to prepare your business for sale. But here's the thing, you should do that from the beginning. The things that you will do to make your business salable will also make it more profitable with less work from you.

1. Recurring Revenue

One of the biggest drivers of the value of a business is recurring revenue. Think about it. When someone buys your business, they base the price on the historical financial performance of the business. One of the buyer's largest risks is that financial performance will not continue. Recurring revenue mitigates a substantial amount of this risk.

If your work is mostly project based, the buyer has to discount the price they are willing to pay because they're assuming that not all of that project work will continue or be replaced. Having long-term clients will help, but project work is not going to be valued as high as recurring revenue.

This leads you to want to have as much retainer or fixed service revenue as possible. You will still likely have project work for some of those clients, and that is okay. In other words, you probably won't ever have a business with 100 percent recurring revenue. That is not what you are shooting for. Depending on your specific business and the industry of your customers, 50 percent would be a good target for recurring revenue.

When the buyer looks at your recurring revenue, they will be looking at your retention. How long do those customers stick with you? Obviously, the longer, the better. They will also look for standardization of service offering. Do you have three core service offerings for recurring revenue, or do you mostly customize your services to each customer? Standardized and fewer offerings will be valued higher than more and varied.

Having standardized service offerings also gives the buyer more assurance that their costs are not going to change. For instance, John Jantsch's company (Duct Tape Marketing) has a marketing agency that acts as a fractional chief marketing officer for other businesses. Companies pay him a monthly amount that covers a menu of services, including monitoring SEO, Google Search, Google Analytics, and social media, providing a quarterly strategy with an execution plan, and then giving the business feedback on their marketing performance. This recurring revenue stream gives him a very nice, salable business.

With customized service offerings, costs vary more, which doesn't give the buyer the assurance that the financial performance is predictable. I know that reducing your options feels wrong. You want to help everyone. I get it. But if you want a valuable business, stay in your lane and focus.

When we implemented EOS, we had to reduce our service offerings significantly. We were simply doing too many things to do them all well. We initially reduced our service offerings to one. After we were laser focused on doing it well and performing, we were able to add two additional service offerings. We tried to have service offerings that covered 100 percent of the target market.

A little bit more on that. We are trying to create a "Star" company as defined by Richard Koch in his book *The Star Principle*. He defines a Star company as one that is growing at 10 percent per year and has at least a 10 percent market share. The 10 percent growth rate is usually not a problem for most businesses. That is not a huge hurdle.

Obtaining a 10 percent market share is significantly more difficult. The trick is to be uber-clear on defining the market. If you want to have a 10 percent market share of marketing agencies, you are going to have to be the size of Ogilvy. Probably not going to happen. If instead, you define your market much more narrowly, you have a chance. For instance, you might be able to have 10 percent market share of marketing agencies serving large animal veterinarians in the US.

The trick is to define your target market, so it is large enough to dominate (10 percent and growing) but *no larger*. The larger the market, the harder it is to dominate. It is better to err on the side of a too small market. Of course, all of this ties neatly into the marketing and pricing we've already discussed in Chapter 4. If you have a well-defined target market, and an awesome solution, you will be able to grow more easily and charge a premium.

If you don't already have a recurring service model in your business, use your creativity to convert an existing service or come up with a new one that is more conducive to recurring billing.

2. Systems

One of the other drivers of value for a business is its dependency on the owner. If you are removed from the business, is the business still as profitable? Referencing the types of buyers above, a cash flow buyer has to have the historical financial results to finance the deal with the bank. If half the revenue goes out the door because you are the only one who can produce it, or because you handle bringing in the work, they're not going to pay for it.

To end this issue, your business must have processes for every critical part of your business. This will include marketing/sales, production, and finance. There may be others, but every business shares these in common.

Fortunately, EOS has processes as one of its key components. Working through EOS, you will learn to document all of your processes so that a competent professional can pick them up and do the work the way that you want it. You do not need detailed procedures showing screenshots for each software, step by step.

Initially preparing these processes is no easy task. They have to be reviewed and updated periodically. Most importantly, they must be followed by all. A procedure that sits unimplemented is useless. When my team initially tackled this task, the person responsible for creating the processes did not involve the team sufficiently. When the procedures were completed, there wasn't buy-in from the people who were going to use them. Consequently, they weren't used, and the whole project was a waste of time.

Individual processes should be no longer than two pages. We're talking high level, don't get lost in the weeds. Once all of the processes are documented, you combine them into one manual that is distributed to all of your team. This allows everyone in your business to know, at a high level, how the business works. Only recently, I had a question from one of my team about how our client onboarding worked. She had been with us for almost two years, so I asked her, "Where do you think you could find that?" She was able to reference Corey's Way (what we call our process manual) and answer her own question.

**Download Sample Process Document at
www.profitfirst4creatives.com/resources**

Creating and documenting processes is not necessarily fun or easy, but it is *fun*damental (see what I did there?). Use your team to assist with individual processes and then simplify and shorten for the whole team to share.

3. Accountability (Organizational) Chart

In order to grow your company, you have to have the right organizational structure. A key component of EOS is traction (actually the name of Wickman's book on EOS). Traction means making progress toward your business goals with your efforts. This is opposed to spinning your wheels, which I felt before implementing EOS (I worked really hard but wasn't going anywhere).

They use several tools to make sure that you are actually getting things done, but it starts with the Accountability Chart. Similar to an organizational chart, an accountability chart primarily defines roles and responsibilities in the business. As was explained to me: When something isn't working, which employee's eyes do you look in for the answer?

I wouldn't recommend trying to create an accountability chart by yourself. You and your team are probably too close to the business and focused on the people that are already in the business to be able to do it effectively. That being said, I have provided several samples on our resources page for various creative industries.

To start, the accountability chart should be designed with the *ideal* structure in mind, not what you currently have. You focus on the roles and responsibilities, not people. That comes later. The accountability chart should be the ideal structure for you to achieve your business goals over the next twelve to eighteen months. And don't worry, it will change frequently. We review ours every year, but often times it changes during the year based upon changing business goals.

> **Download a sample accountability chart at www.profitfirst4creatives.com/resources**

Once you have the Accountability Chart completed, you can move to putting actual people into it.

4. Team

People are another of the key components of EOS. Once you have the Accountability Chart created, you can then look at filling those positions (or boxes). When you look at the three to five most important roles and responsibilities for a box, who best fills that role? It may be someone on your team currently or it may be someone not yet hired. In many cases, a person may sit in multiple boxes, but only one person per box. Remember, we need to know who to talk to when something isn't working. Can't have two people responsible, because then no one is responsible.

When putting people in boxes (that sounds bad, doesn't it?), you want to consider three things: Do they *get* it, do they *want* it, and do they have the *capacity*? The easiest is *get it*, which means, do they understand the roles and responsibilities for their job/box?

Want is probably the hardest to figure out, because only that person knows whether they really want it. They probably aren't going to tell you that they don't want it because they want to be a team player, and they don't want to be fired. But if someone doesn't want the job, they will never be good at it.

As I mentioned earlier, my brother was in charge of finance for several years. He did it because I asked him to, and he was the best person for the job (that we had). But he didn't want it. I don't know if he didn't want it from the outset, but it became clear over time that he didn't want to do it, because he didn't do a good job. It wasn't because he didn't have the capacity to do it, he just didn't like it. Be very careful with making sure that people want their roles.

Capacity is simply: Do they have the time, skills, and/or experience to do the job? If they want the job, and they don't have the skills, can you educate them? If they don't have the experience, can they work under or with someone else to gain that experience? If they don't have the time, well that's another matter altogether.

In many small businesses, like ours and yours, people have to fill multiple boxes. We simply aren't big enough to be able to have different people in each box and still make a profit. When people sit in multiple boxes it can lead to a constraint on time. Eventually this will mean that they can't handle all of the roles and responsibilities in all of the boxes they fill. This will lead to some difficult conversations and decisions. You will have to decide which roles are most important and prioritize those.

Eventually, you will get to a point where people will be in fewer and fewer boxes and will be able to focus more. We created a box on our leadership team for human resources, because of the importance of people to our organization. The problem was that for over a year, the person sitting in that box also sat in three other boxes. Because she didn't have the time, the bigger picture, long-term things of the HR box went undone. With a lot of work, delegating, coaching, and education, we were able to remove her from those boxes and she is now able to focus on her HR role. Once she was able to allocate time and energy to it, she started blowing the doors off!

More than anything I've seen, your team will drive your growth success. Each member has to be a cultural fit (on the right bus), and have to get it, want it, and have the capacity do the role they have been assigned (in the right seat).

Summary

This chapter is not for most of you, I understand, but I would be remiss if I didn't include my hard-learned experience on these subjects. We discussed navigating a business with a partner, and how to use a forecast and a rolling income statement to project cash flow and monitor traction of your business plan. Finally, we discussed how to grow your business using the Entrepreneurial Operating System and how to build a business to sell.

Here are the action items should you proceed:

- If you have a business partner or are considering one, get with your attorney and create legal agreements.
- Create a forecast for your business for the next twelve months.
- Begin using trailing twelve- and three-month income statements to monitor how well your business decisions are doing.
- Implement Entrepreneurial Operating System in your business. Start with the accountability chart and build the right team.
- Systemize everything.
- Focus on adding recurring revenue.

Final thoughts coming up…

Chapter 10:
Final Thoughts

As I've said multiple times, Profit First works 100 percent of the time that it is implemented, correctly. The process is simple and straightforward:

1. Open the five bank accounts (Deposit, Profit, Taxes, Owner's Compensation, Operating Expenses) (Chapter 2).
2. Do an Instant Profit Assessment (Chapter 3).
3. Use your Instant Profit Assessment to establish your Target Allocation Percentages (TAPs) (Chapters 3 and 5).
4. Deposit all of your income into the Deposit account (Chapter 2).
5. Periodically (e.g., twice a month) transfer money from the Deposit account to the other accounts using your TAPs (Chapter 2).
6. Distribute your profit to yourself once a quarter (Chapter 2).
7. Evaluate your TAPs for the next quarter (Chapter 2).

But you can find that in the *Profit First* book. What I really want you to take from this book is this:

You don't have to compromise your creativity to make a profit. Creativity and profitability are complementary!

If you understand and believe this, you can use Profit First to create the business of your dreams—one that is profitable, enjoyable, and not soul-sucking. You will have more time and love what you do. In fact, I'm so convinced of this, that if you have attempted to implement

Profit First, and find it doesn't work for you, I will volunteer my time to help you diagnose the problem.

From what we learned about human behavior from Pareto, we know only a small percentage of creatives will purchase this book. A small percentage of those will actually read the book all the way through. And then a small percentage of those will *do* something with it.

You've finished the book, which puts you in rare air, maybe top 10-20 percent of all creatives. Congratulations! Now what are you going to do with it?

I poured everything I could put into this book in the hopes of giving you value, but now you have to use that knowledge and experience. *You* have to do it; no one else can do it for you, but I, and the other Profit First Professionals, will be there to guide and encourage you.

If you haven't already, go set up your Profit savings account. Take 1 percent of your next deposit and put it in there. Don't touch or even look at the account, just keep making deposits each time you have a deposit in your checking account. Do that for thirteen weeks (one quarter). When those thirteen weeks are over, you will be surprised by how much is in that account. I promise.

After completing this exercise, then you can take the next step. My suggestion would be to reach out to a us at Core—or another Profit First Professional—to assist, but if you want to go it alone, do an Instant Profit Assessment to see where your finances are. Decide on your Target Allocation Percentages for the next thirteen weeks. Maybe it is just raising that 1 percent to 2 percent. You don't have to set up the other accounts yet if you don't want to.

I know that as you see your profit increase in that account, you will be hooked. Eventually you will need to set up the remaining accounts and either get your current accountant on board with Profit First or hire a Profit First Professional. You will need them not just to customize Profit First for your business, but you will need the support when you inevitably run into a problem. You don't have to go on this journey alone.

And once you have Profit First properly implemented in your business, the sky is the limit. Your creativity is going to go through the roof, and so will your profits. As you delve deeper into understanding your client's total problem, developing a novel complete solution, and charging for it, your revenue will rise and so will your profit.

Make sure you make time to implement the remaining process besides Profit First in your business: Bookkeeping, Tax Compliance, and Payroll. Don't be dissuaded by setbacks and challenges. I've outlined the most common you are likely to encounter, and told you how to overcome them, but if you run into something you can't solve, I am always available to assist you however I can. My email is profitfirst@coregroupus.com and my cell phone is 405-212-4183. Please reach out with questions or concerns.

Now, go get 'em. I'm rooting for you!

Christian Brim

About the Author

Christian Brim is a Certified Public Accountant and Certified Management Accountant with over 25 years of working with small businesses to grow their businesses profitably. Heavily influenced by a family riches to rags experience in his formative years, Christian has dedicated his life's work to helping entrepreneurs have businesses that work for them.

Printed in Great Britain
by Amazon